Write
THIS WAY

How **MODELING** Transforms the Writing Classroom

By Kelly Boswell

🍎 Maupin House *by*
capstone·
professional

Write This Way: How Modeling Transforms the Writing Classroom
By Kelly Boswell

© Copyright 2016. Kelly Boswell. All rights reserved.

Cover Design: Sandra D'Antonio
Book Design: Jodi Pedersen

Photo Credits: Shutterstock: Elena Schweitzer, cover, MarcelClemens, 101

Library of Congress Cataloging-in-Publication Data

Cataloging-in-publication information is on file with the Library of Congress.

978-1-62521-932-9 (pbk.)

978-1-62521-942-8 (eBook PDF)

978-1-4966-0305-0 (eBook)

Maupin House publishes professional resources for K-12 educators. Contact us for tailored, in-school training or to schedule an author for a workshop or conference. Visit www.maupinhouse.com for free lesson plan downloads.

Maupin House Publishing, Inc. by Capstone Professional
1710 Roe Crest Drive
North Mankato, MN 56003
www.maupinhouse.com
888-262-6135
info@maupinhouse.com

To my parents, Tom and Hazel Jay,
who modeled how to dream big,
love well, and risk the ocean.

"My father didn't tell me how to live;
he lived, and he let me watch him do it."
— Clarence Budington Kelland

ACKNOWLEDGMENTS

It has been an honor to work with the dedicated and talented group of educators at Capstone Professional, and I am grateful for their support each step of the way. My editor, Karen Soll, was a master at providing genuine and gentle feedback to me while I found my voice as a writer. Emily Raij made the final stages possible with her wisdom and support. The design team created a cover that captured the essence of the book in just one picture. And Dave Willette provided smart and savvy guidance along the way. Thank you for all that you did to make this book a reality. It has been a privilege to work with each of you.

Years ago, Tony Stead came to our school district to present a workshop on nonfiction reading and writing. I laughed until I cried, filled dozens of pages with notes, and left with a renewed energy to teach. I am honored that he contributed the foreword for this book. Thank you so much, Tony.

Lynnette Brent, one of the kindest, smartest, and most genuine people I know: I feel richer each time I interact with you. Thank you for opening many doors of opportunity to me.

I stand on the shoulders of many researchers, authors, and teachers who have championed best practices in writing instruction. Some of them I have never met, and some of them I cherish as dear friends. Each of them has shaped the way I view writing and teach children. I owe an immeasurable debt of gratitude to Donald Graves, Don Murray, Lucy Calkins, Richard Allington, Vicki Spandel, Dr. Mary Howard, Penny Kittle, Kelly Gallagher, Tom Newkirk, Harvey "Smokey" Daniels, Regie Routman, and Linda Hoyt.

A very special thank you to Tamara Ward, teacher extraordinaire, for contributing photos, writing samples, and mentor text suggestions, and for being a constant source of support and strength. The next latte is definitely on me!

A huge "thank you" also goes out to Judi Hewitt and the fearless teachers and students at Creston Elementary School. Thank you for opening your classrooms (and your hearts) to me. The work you do is a model for what's possible. We could all learn big lessons from your small school.

To Michele Beitel, first-grade teacher, reader, writer, and thinker: Thank you for sharing your classroom and your stories with me. Each time I'm in your classroom, I learn more. Thank you for being a constant voice for common sense and best practice. And, Sharon Navas, principal at Meadowlark Elementary, thank you for supporting the work that your students and teachers do at Meadowlark each day. I'm so glad that our paths have crossed.

Thank you to Jill Bute and Cary Griffith for sharing the delightful writing samples from your children. Your children's voices shine through.

To my sisters, Ginger Jay and Tamara Ward, amazing teachers and advocates for children: I am in constant awe of what you do day in and day out for the learners in your care. Thank you for your words of wisdom and love.

During my career, I was fortunate enough to work for two incredible administrators. Sandra Wrightson supported my first fledgling efforts at teaching writing. When I was a first-year teacher, she saw potential and sent me to a four-day workshop presented by Vicki Spandel. What followed was the beginning of a lifelong love affair with writing instruction. Zan Hess evaluated my teaching with the utmost care and encouraged me to keep reading, writing, and wondering. Both of these administrators have shaped me personally and professionally, and I am in their debt.

I have been blessed to work alongside some of the finest educators who so generously shared their wisdom, their "go-to" lessons, and their keen observations of student learning: Jan McCall, Sarah Dunkin, Kerry Bishop, Tasha Radford, Kristy Castor, Michelle King, Renee Niepoky, Leslie Whitmore, Sherri Nissen, Heidi Freeman, and Melissa Mayes. Thank you.

Thank you to Tina Pletan, Erin Jacobson, Rhonda Goetz, Tara Hofmann, and all of the instructional coaches from Bismarck School District in North Dakota. You encouraged me to write this book when it was just an idea floating around in my head, and you have cheered my efforts ever since.

To April Willard, esteemed colleague and friend: You are a voice for best practices and lifelong learning.

To Carson and Brady, my little warriors. You make life fun and keep things real. Wherever you go, go with all of your heart.

Finally, I could not have written this book without the love and tenacious support of my husband, Cory. I cannot think of anyone else I would rather do life with.

TABLE OF CONTENTS

FOREWORD

Finally! Not just another book about how to teach writing, but one that targets the power of modeled writing. What a delight it is to read this professional resource that highlights the importance of this strategy as the cornerstone to successful teaching and learning of the writing process.

Explicitly showing students what writers do when they compose has long been the back burner to modeling reading in the language arts classroom. While we eagerly model the reading process through read-alouds, modeled writing is not usually a focused and regular part of classroom instruction. Most teachers themselves are not writers and therefore find it difficult to demonstrate to students what is involved in crafting a well-thought-out piece. If we want students to be successful writers, we as teachers have to be masters of the pen and model our endeavors on a regular basis. We have to adopt the pedagogy that Kelly so beautifully describes throughout the book of "show— don't tell."

This book has so much to offer! It is a delight the way Kelly highlights the importance of oral language to elevate students' comprehension of the writing process. Her wonderful anecdotes of classroom dialogue demonstrate the importance that listening and speaking play in heightening a student's ability to reach a greater understanding. Her term, "Make Your Thinking Transparent," is a reminder that we should not assume students are internalizing the demonstration we provide.

Kelly's enlightening and refreshing ideas in "The Courage to Revise" and "Give Audience and Purpose Center Stage" in Chapter 5 are welcomed. Revision has long been the Achilles' heel in the successful writing classroom. Kelly so seamlessly guides us through targeted ways to get our students to elevate the quality of their writing through purposeful revision. Too often our students write with no audience in mind, therefore making the revision process a tiresome and painful affair. When writers compose with an audience in mind, their aptitude and desire to revise is elevated, bringing richness to their word usage, sentence fluency, and voice.

Having worked closely with Kelly before and knowing her passion for nonfiction, I was eager to read her suggestions for modeling different genres and text types. Her suggestions in Chapters 5 and 7 give careful consideration to teaching students how to work with different genres, an area in which most teachers struggle. While there is a certain comfort level in modeling how to write personal narratives, showing students how to write opinion pieces, descriptions, and explanations is not the norm, especially in the early years. This is partially because we as teachers are not versed with the structure and features of these text types. Kelly's advice of "Don't let your own writing difficulties keep you from engaging in modeled writing" is heartening. By taking risks as teachers, we show students that we as adults often struggle with writing in different genres, thus encouraging them to also be risk takers. Through fearlessly facing and overcoming challenges as writers ourselves, we get a better idea of the struggles children face, allowing us to become more in-tuned mentors. One must first climb the mountain before advising others on how to successfully accomplish the journey.

Kelly's advice in Chapter 6 on using well-crafted mentor texts as models for writing is wonderful. So often, we use beautifully crafted pieces of literature as part of reader's workshop but never consider the impacts of these texts as models for writing. Kelly's advice in using high-quality literature for both reading and writing is a multi-lens approach that warrants applause.

This is a must-read for every teacher. It is insightful, beautifully written, and extremely poignant at a time when the Common Core Standards urge us to give students the tools for writing for a variety of purposes in a multitude of forms. Kelly provides us with the scaffolds to achieve these goals. In Chapter 3, Kelly shares "a little secret" and I'm going to let you in on a secret as well. This book is a rare gem and one that I will constantly revisit to elevate the impact of my own modeling. Kelly, your message is clear: By becoming a constant and reflective writer in front of my students, I am able to not only raise the quality of their writing, but also their joy in picking up the pen and being writers for life. Kelly, you're a master!

Thank you!
— Tony Stead

Chapter 1:

THE POWER OF MODELING

> "Nothing, absolutely *nothing* you will ever do as a teacher
> will be more powerful than modeling writing in
> front of your students."

> — Vicki Spandel

Years ago, I decided to learn to knit. So I did what any self-respecting would-be knitter does—I marched myself down to my local library and checked out a book that promised to make me a knitter by Chapter 3.

With needles and yarn in hand, I perused the pages and carefully studied the illustrations and diagrams, and yet I quickly discovered that, in this case, a picture was *not* worth a thousand words. I simply could not make my fingers and yarn look like the ones shown on page 2. I could see the picture of the needle going through the small hole but, try as I may, I could not "cast on." It didn't take me long to realize that the words and pictures in this book (or any book) couldn't teach me all that I needed to know in order to knit. I needed someone to *show* me how.

I phoned Grandma Wilson, my husband's grandmother, and asked if she'd kindly clear her social calendar and teach me to knit. After my repeated promises of copious quantities of chocolate as payment, she gladly obliged.

On a sunny Saturday morning, we gathered our materials and made ourselves comfortable on the couch. Grandma began by asking me to simply *watch* her. She showed me how she tied a slipknot, and then she cast the first few stitches. I watched. I listened. I tried it on my own. Several times throughout the morning, Grandma placed her hands over mine and guided them as I attempted a stitch. Then she released me to try it on my own. Each time I would mangle my yarn into an unmanageable mess, she would softly say, "Okay, let's see what we've got here," quietly unravel the knots, and ask me to watch her again.

After a few more Saturdays (and heaps more chocolate), I was starting to get the hang of it. I was knitting. Pretty much. (Okay, in truth, I learned enough to make several scarves that I gave as gifts and my family wore for a few days as a show of support and immense kindness, but you get the point.)

Years later, I realized that Grandma Wilson had done what many effective teachers do: She had modeled the task. She had explicitly demonstrated and shown me what a proficient knitter is thinking and doing when she knits. Those mornings with Grandma Wilson were worth much more than anything I could have learned from a book.

If you think about it, modeling plays an important role in how the human brain learns almost anything. Infants and toddlers watch their caregivers walk, talk, and eat with a spoon. Piano students notice and note the way the instructor's hands are placed on the keys when playing scales. Tennis players watch and listen as the coach demonstrates how to serve the ball. Student teachers observe a master teacher before teaching lessons on their own.

Collins, Brown, and Newman (1989) call this *cognitive apprenticeship*. Through this apprenticeship, processes that are usually carried out internally (i.e., reading, playing piano, driving, etc.) are externalized so the learner can see how an expert completes the task.

Modeling is said to be one of the most effective of all teaching strategies (Pearson and Fielding, 1991). This is especially true when it comes to writing. Research has consistently found that teachers who engage in writing experiences themselves can connect more authentically with students during the writing process (Cremin, 2006; Kaplan, 2008). Fisher and Frey (2003) found that writing fluency improved significantly when teachers modeled their own writing.

In 2012, Sharon Zumbrunn and Keegan Krause wrote an article that appeared in *The Reading Teacher*. In the article, seven leading authorities in the field of writing were interviewed and asked to share their beliefs about effective writing instruction. Zumbrunn and Krause wrote, "...(leaders) stressed that writing teachers need to be writers themselves and, as Thomas Newkirk said, 'know from the inside out what writing is like.'"

If we want kindergartners to gather information from resources, it's imperative that teachers *show* them how. Likewise, if fifth graders are going to dig into the courageous and sometimes difficult work of planning, editing, and revising, they must have the opportunity to tune in and notice the things that other writers do when they plan, edit, and revise.

In the same article, Jerome Harste (2012) recommended the following: "If I were to give a tip to teachers, I'd tell them to take out a sheet of paper and start writing. I'd also tell them to share what they write with students. I think we (as teachers) provide the type of demonstration that students need to see and be around. There's power in making yourself as vulnerable as the students you're teaching."

The Common Core State Standards, or CCSS (2010), and most state standards require high-quality research and writing from even the youngest of children. These standards ask writers at every grade level to create pieces of narrative, informative or explanatory, and opinion writing in order to be prepared for the kinds of writing we do as lifelong writers.

As I read the CCSS, I notice one phrase that appears over and over: "*with guidance and support from adults.*" For example, one of the standards for kindergarten states, "*With guidance and support from adults*, recall information from experiences or gather information from provided sources to answer a question" (CCSS.ELA-LITERACY.W.K.8). In fifth grade, one of the standards reads, "*With guidance and support from peers and adults*, develop and strengthen writing as needed by planning, revising, editing, rewriting, or trying a new approach" (CCSS.ELA-LITERACY.W.5.5).

It's clear, isn't it? If we want kindergartners to gather information from resources, it's imperative that teachers *show* them how. Likewise, if fifth graders are going to dig into the courageous and sometimes difficult work of planning, editing, and revising, they must have the opportunity to tune in and notice the things that other writers do when they plan, edit, and revise.

As writing teachers, we often neglect the powerful strategy of modeling in our classrooms. We use mentor texts as a way to examine what other authors do in their writing, but we rarely demonstrate our own thinking and processes. Donald Graves (2013), a longtime advocate for modeled writing, said "Students can go a lifetime and never see another person write, much less show them how to write. Yet, it would be unheard of for an artist to not show her students how to use oils by painting on her own canvas, or for a ceramist not to demonstrate how to throw clay on a wheel and shape the material himself."

So what if we crafted a piece of writing *in front* of our students, showing them how a proficient writer thinks and what a proficient writer does? What if we gave students a window into our thinking and allowed them to see the reality and messiness of our own writing process? What if we made ourselves vulnerable and took risks as writers—and what if we did that in front of our students?

I believe there is immense power in giving students a peek into the mind and processes of another writer. In fact, I believe that modeled writing could be called "a 10-minute makeover" for the classroom. If, every day, we took five to 10 minutes to model our own thinking and writing before asking students to write, we could transform our students into successful writers.

An anchor chart that we made for a mini-lesson or a list of writing features projected on an interactive whiteboard simply cannot take the place of an authentic piece of writing that is crafted on the spot. When I model, I'm showing students what I do before I write, while I'm writing, and when I finish a piece of writing.

Modeling also strengthens our students' knowledge of:

- writing behaviors,

- different types of text,

- the writing process,

- story structures,

- how writing helps us and enriches our everyday life, and

- the vocabulary that writers use to talk about writing.

> If, every day, we took five to 10 minutes to model our own thinking and writing before asking students to write, we could transform our students into successful writers.

A Few Clarifications about Writing Instruction

Before we continue, allow me to make a few clarifications. In my workshops with teachers, I notice there is some confusion about what modeled writing is. Many teachers confuse modeled writing with other kinds of writing instruction found in classrooms. So let me begin by first explaining the difference between modeled writing and other writing experiences.

Modeled writing should not be confused with *shared writing*. A shared writing experience invites students to collaborate with the teacher to create a piece of writing. In a shared writing experience, the teacher holds the pen, but students jump in, give suggestions, and interact with the teacher as he or she writes.

Modeled writing also differs from *interactive writing*. In an interactive writing experience, teachers and students work together to decide what words, phrases, and sentences should be included in the piece, but now individual students are holding the pen and doing the actual drafting.

Shared writing and interactive writing are both effective scaffolds that support student writers, and they have a place in the writing classroom. Both experiences provide an opportunity to share ideas, collaborate, and create a piece of strong writing by working with other writers. Shared writing and interactive writing make it possible for all students to create a high-quality piece while raising the expectation for what is possible. Although shared writing and interactive writing help promote writing, I believe that the real transformation in our writing classrooms occurs when teachers engage in modeled writing.

Modeled writing is unique in that the teacher is doing all or most of the thinking and talking and all of the writing. In a modeled writing experience, students are invited to tune in and notice the things that the writer is doing, but they don't offer suggestions or ideas for improving the piece. Instead, students listen and observe as the teacher plans, makes choices, researches, drafts, rereads, edits, evaluates, or revises. The teacher makes his or her thinking transparent while students observe. (See Fig. 1.1.)

Fig 1.1

	Teacher	Students	Example of teacher language
Shared writing	Asks for ideas and suggestions from students Holds the pen and does the actual writing Writes, stops, and rereads often to see how the writing sounds	Share ideas and suggestions for what should be written Reread to see how the piece sounds	*What do we think about this lead?* *Who has an idea about how we could start this piece?*
Interactive writing	Guides students as they think of words, phrases, or sentences to add to a piece of writing Supports individual students as they add to the piece of writing	Suggest words, phrases, or sentences that can be added to the piece Hold the pen and do the actual writing Reread to see how the piece sounds	*So we agreed that we wanted to add this sentence here, "Bears are excellent climbers." Who would like to come up and add that sentence to our piece?*
Modeled writing	Thinks aloud Writes a portion of a piece Stops to reread and sometimes revises while drafting Does all or most of the talking	Watch and listen Notice what the teacher is thinking and doing as he or she writes	*I want to speak directly to my reader here to add a little voice and interest to my writing. I'm thinking I could write….* *Or I could write….* *I like the way my first idea sounded. Watch me as I add that to my writing.*

Blaze the Trail

My husband and I both love to hike, and we'd love nothing better than to pass this love of the outdoors on to our two young sons. So several times each summer, we pack enough snacks to feed a small village and head for the hills.

When we hike as a family, my husband is usually assigned to "blaze the trail." He goes ahead of us and we trod behind. As he hikes, he will often look back at us and say, "Hey, watch your step on this rock. It's slippery," or "Step over this log like this."

Our rationale is that if the boys watch my husband explore the trail first and learn from what he is encountering, it will help them to navigate the trail more successfully and actually increase their love of hiking. In short, it allows my husband to experience the trail first as a hiker and then as a guide.

What if we approached the teaching of writing with the same principle? What if we were willing to "blaze the trail" by experiencing writing tasks first as a writer and then as a guide? When we model our own thinking and writing for students, we are doing just that. We are saying: *I know what the path before you is like. I've been there. Let me help you by sharing what I've discovered.*

In order to see what this looks like in the classroom, let's examine two variations of the same writing task.

Teacher A gives students an assignment. Students are asked to create a travel brochure about a state of their choosing. She makes a list of features that must be included in each travel brochure and explains that students will start by researching and collecting important facts about their states. She points out the basket of books that they can use when gathering their facts and reminds them to write down facts in their own words rather than simply copying the facts that they find in the book.

Teacher B explains that over the next few weeks, everyone will be researching and creating a travel brochure about a state. He passes out several travel brochures that he has collected from a local travel agency and asks partners to think about and answer the question: *What makes a good brochure?*

As he listens to several pairs share, he creates a chart called "Qualities of a Good Travel Brochure." He and his students work together to create a list of features (colorful photographs, lists of attractions, a section about the weather, etc.).

After each student has chosen the state that he or she will write about, Teacher B chooses a state that has not been selected by anyone else. Over the next few days, before students began researching, Teacher B takes 10 minutes to show the students how he reads a short section of text and then jots down words or phrases to capture important facts about his state. Once he's collected several facts, he thinks out loud and explicitly demonstrates how he uses the words and phrases to create interesting and inviting sentences to include in his travel brochure.

I predict that the students in Teacher A's classroom will struggle. Without explicit teaching and modeling about *how* to read, research, and write, many students will simply do what they've always done— copy facts from the resources provided. The readers and writers in Teacher A's classroom will likely become confused over the process and might simply give up and look for something more interesting to do. Those who do complete a brochure likely won't match Teacher A's expectations. Teacher A *assigned* a writing task, but she didn't *teach* students how to engage in the reading and writing processes necessary for the task.

On the other hand, I predict that the students in Teacher B's classroom will jump right in and experience success! The students in this classroom have been given the opportunity to examine the kind of information that is included in a quality travel brochure. The teacher has explicitly modeled how to locate information, read, take notes, and then turn those notes into running text. They've seen how an adult reader, writer, and thinker approaches the work. Teacher B hasn't simply *assigned* a writing task; he has *shown* students how to engage with the resources to create high-quality work.

It's clear, isn't it? Before we ask students to do something, we should be willing to do it first. So before we ask our students to create a persuasive poster that teaches others about the importance of daily exercise, we should demonstrate how *we* would create a poster on a similar topic, such as eating more fruits and vegetables. If our student writers are going to be crafting a book review on one of their favorite books, we should show them how *we* write one using one of *our*

> Without explicit teaching and modeling about *how* to read, research, and write, many students will simply do what they've always done— copy facts from the resources provided.

favorite books. These explicit demonstrations allow students to see how another writer completes the task. They also help students see what's possible in their own writing. We blaze the trail and invite them to come join us!

The bottom line is this: As writing instructors, it's imperative that we write. Think about it. If you want your child to learn ballet, you wouldn't sign him or her up for lessons taught by someone who doesn't dance. There's a reason why a swim instructor wears a bathing suit and is in the water. Learning to write (like learning to dance, swim, or knit) happens best when someone comes alongside us and *shows* us how it's done.

Throughout the next eight chapters, you'll find tips, sample models, tools, and stories from the classroom to help you unleash the power of modeled writing in your classroom. I'll serve as your guide as I share the triumphs and the tribulations from my own journey as a teacher of writing. Sprinkled throughout the book, you'll find a plethora of examples of teacher language that you can use as you make your own thinking and writing visible to your students. In Chapter 7, I've created several sample mini-lessons that can be used "as is" or tweaked to match the needs of the learners in your classroom. Finally, in the Appendix, you'll find reproducible templates that will help you as you plan for modeled writing and work with student writers.

As you read this book, I hope you'll feel a nudge to begin the daily practice of thinking and writing out loud in front of your students. I think you'll find it's a powerful way to transform your writing classroom and give your student writers the tools and the confidence that they need to soar!

Chapter 2:
THE DIFFERENCE BETWEEN MODELING AND EXPLAINING

"When you write with your students, you show them
what writing is for. You show them the 'why' of
writing and how to negotiate the journey from
the germ of an idea to final copy."

— Donald Graves

Recently, I taught my son how to tie his shoes. He and I sat on our living room floor, each of us with a shoe in our hands and determination in our eyes. I modeled. He struggled. I offered encouragement. He practiced. I untied the knots and wiped away the tears. With the clenched fists of frustration, he took the laces in hand and tried and tried and tried again. I was reminded how hard it is to learn something new—especially something that requires so much focus (and fine-motor control).

Later, as I reflected on our shoe-tying lessons, I wondered: *What if I had simply explained how to tie shoes without actually showing him how? I could have just said: Okay, Carson, here's what a shoe looks like when it's tied. Someone picked up the laces and made an "x" with them. Then they brought the lace that's on top around and through and pulled it tight. Next, they picked up one of the laces and made a "bunny ear." They did the same with the other one and then they made the "bunny ears" into an "x." Finally, they brought one of the "bunny ears" around and through the hole and pulled both of the "ears" tight. Okay, give it a shot!*

Had I done that, I'm guessing that I would have spent the afternoon untying many more knots and wiping away countless more tears. Most of us, when we learn something new, need more than explanations—

we need someone to explicitly *show* us how it's done. If we as "mature" learners need demonstrations, just imagine how much more the children in our classroom need them.

A few years ago, I observed a lesson in a second-grade classroom. The well-meaning teacher wanted her students to include a table of contents in the students' informational writing. She gathered her students together and said: *Today, I want you to add a table of contents to your books. Let's look at the table of contents in this Big Book. When you make a table of contents, you list all the sections in your book and then you tell your reader what page that section begins on. See? This section called "Speedy Sharks" starts on page 13, so the author put little dots after "Speedy Sharks" and then wrote the number "13." So, today, let's all try and add a table of contents to our books, just like this author did.*

When the students returned to their desks, many of them had difficulty. Some were able to look back at the table of contents in the Big Book and begin to make their own, but most of the children weren't sure how to get started. And few of them understood *why* they were making a table of contents in the first place.

The outcome would have been far different if she would have modeled. She could have said something like this: *The author of this Big Book included a table of contents. As a reader, I can use the table of contents to easily navigate through this book and find the information I want quickly. For example, if I want to find out how fast sharks can swim, I can turn to page 13—the chapter called "Speedy Swimmers" starts on that page. See how the table of contents can be a helpful tool to guide you to find what you need? This is something we should think about including in our own writing to help our readers. Today, I'm going to show you the things I do to add a table of contents to my writing. Watch me, and notice what I do.*

I have three sections in my piece about caves: "Kinds of Caves," "Animal Life Inside Caves," and "How to Explore a Cave." First, I'll write "Table of Contents" at the top of the page. Now, over on the left side of the page, I'll write down the titles of the three sections. My reader will want to know what page to turn to, so I'll make a line of dots like this, and then I'll write the page number. The section called "Kinds of Caves" starts on page 3, so I'll write a "3" here. My next section is called "Animal Life Inside Caves." As I look at my piece, I notice that section begins on page 5, so I'll write a "5" here. I'll continue adding a page

"7" here because it shows the reader where "How to Explore a Cave" starts. Did you see how I did that? Did you see how I wrote the words "Table of Contents" at the top of my page? Did you see how I thought about the sections in my book and then I listed them on the left-hand side? Did you notice how I made the little dots and then added the page numbers? Today, try adding a table of contents to your own piece of writing. Your reader will thank you!

Once students understand why a table of contents is important to readers and they see and hear another writer create one, they are in a much better position to try it on their own—and they are much more likely to experience success.

So what's the difference between *explaining* and *modeling*?

When we *explain*, we...	When we *model*, we...
• summarize the writing activity. • show the finished piece of writing. • talk about what we *did* and the decisions we made.	• act out the process we want students to do. • create the writing *in front* of the student. • think out loud *while* we are writing.

The biggest difference between explaining and modeling can be seen (and heard) in the language that is used for each.

When we *explain*, we might say:	When we *model*, we might say:
In this piece, I decided to open with a question to make it more interesting. See how I put a question right here?	I'm ready to begin my piece about sharks, and I think I'll do what I've seen other informative writers do—I'll open with a question. Let's see…I could write, "Do you think you know everything about sharks?" That's okay, but let me see what else I can write to make a reader want to read my piece. I could say, "Have you ever wondered why sharks are the most feared creatures in the ocean?" I like that because I think many of my readers may wonder about that. Watch me as I get that down on the page.
Look at the sentences I wrote. Some sentences are long and some are short. When we write, we want some variety in the length of our sentences.	I want my writing to include short, long, and medium-length sentences. When I do that, it makes my writing more interesting and fun to read aloud. My first sentence is pretty long, so I think I'll write a short sentence next. Maybe I could write a sentence with just two words. Let's see…I could write, "Night approaches." Or, I could say, "Sun fades." I think I like "Sun fades." Watch me as I write that. Now I have a long sentence and a short sentence.
I spoke directly to my readers here. That helps draw readers in and makes them want to keep reading.	I noticed that some writers speak directly to their reader, and I want to try that too. In this section of my piece about the stripes on tigers, I could say, "If you were brave enough to get close to a group of tigers, you might notice that no two tigers have the same stripe pattern." I like that. Watch me as I get that down. Okay, I want to keep speaking directly to my reader, so next I think I'll say, "And if you were really brave and wanted to shave a tiger, you would see that the stripe pattern is on the skin too."

When it comes to learning how to write, students need someone to demonstrate, rather than simply explain. Students don't come to us knowing how to choose a topic, craft an inviting lead, edit a piece of work, or spell a tricky word. They need us to *show* them how. When you model instead of explain part of the process to students, they see how it should be done, understand why it's important, and can mimic the process in their own writing.

Chapter 3:

THE WRITER IN ALL OF US

"One of the most powerful ways for students to grow as writers is to watch you write—to observe you plan, think, compose, revise, and edit right in front of them, pretty much off the cuff."

— Regie Routman

As a workshop presenter throughout the United States, I am often on airplanes. As a matter of course, my seatmate and I will begin chatting and eventually the conversation will turn to our work. After listening to me explain what it is that I do, he or she will usually exclaim, "Oh, you're a writer!"—to which I will mutter something like, "No, no. Well…I have done some writing, but I'm not a *writer*."

I am a published author, and I still don't see myself as a writer. Why?

I think it's because I have a distorted picture in my mind of what a writer looks like and what a writer does. When I visualize a "writer," I picture someone who is much more sophisticated and more intelligent than me. In my mind, a writer is someone who sips cappuccino and keeps a dream journal. She takes long walks and spends hours in her well-appointed, book-lined office typing wildly.

I don't think I am alone in my perception of writers. In my workshops with teachers, I often ask participants to raise their hands if they consider themselves readers. Invariably, many hands go up. Then I say, "Now raise your hand if you consider yourself a writer." In most cases, only two or three hands are raised.

For some reason, in our minds, we have much higher standards in place for someone to be considered a writer. It's as if we believe that almost anyone can become a reader, but it takes someone truly gifted to be a writer.

Is this what keeps many of us from writing in front of our students—this unrealistic view of what a writer is and what a writer does? Perhaps it's this distorted picture in our heads that keeps us from plugging into the power of modeling and letting it transform the writers in our classroom.

So let me set the record straight, just in case you are wondering: You are a writer. Yes, *you*. You might not be publishing journal articles or writing children's books, but you write. You are a writer.

Pause for a moment and think about the last five pieces of writing you have crafted this week. Perhaps you wrote a parent newsletter or plans for a substitute teacher. Have you written an e-mail? Jotted down a to-do list or grocery list? Crafted a status update, a tweet, or a text?

Webster's Dictionary defines "writer" as "one who writes." So that should settle it. You are a writer. I am a writer too. We write every day. We write for very specific purposes and for very specific audiences. We write to inform, to instruct, and to remember. We write to respond to something we've read or eaten or purchased. We write to voice an opinion or communicate an emotion. The key to transforming the writing classroom is to make our writing (and thinking) visible for our students—through modeling.

Silence the Internal Critic

Some of you might be thinking, "Okay, I like the idea of modeling. And, yes, I do write, so I guess I am a writer, but…I'm not a good writer."

It's true that many of us carry loads of self-doubt when it comes to our ability to write. Our past experiences, both positive and negative, can shape our beliefs about our writing ability.

I recently asked a group of teachers to reflect on their own experiences as a student writer and the feedback they received. Here are a few of their comments:

- "I would say throughout middle and high school, I only received negative feedback. It was usually in summative form, as the final grade was already recorded, and I had no chance to go back and revise anything."

- "In middle school I had to write reports, and I remember being so terrified because I was afraid of doing them wrong. I didn't know how to write a report and wasn't taught how. I remember getting marks all over my work, fixing my grammar, spelling, and handwriting."

- "The only feedback I can remember was that I overused commas and was too wordy. I needed to get to the point."

Can you relate to these teachers? Perhaps some of us can remember a few positive and encouraging comments from a writing teacher, but I'm guessing that many of us can vividly recall negative (and generally unhelpful) feedback.

John Kaag, in an article written for *The New York Times*, says, "Genuine criticism, the type that leaves an indelible mark on you as a writer, also leaves an existential imprint on you as a person" (2014). It's important for us to realize that negative feedback impacts us as writers and writing teachers. And, for some of us, it prevents us from making our writing public. It keeps us from modeling.

It doesn't have to be that way. The truth is, you don't have to be a stellar writer to engage in modeled writing. The writing that we do in front of our students doesn't need to be perfect. Rather, it should show that we are growing as writers. Our students should see and hear us striving to become better, studying other authors, and taking some risks. We can't expect our students to stretch themselves as writers if they haven't seen us do the same! And, we can't expect our students to be vulnerable if we're not willing to be vulnerable ourselves.

My encouragement to you is this: Set aside any negative feedback that you've received as a writer. Silence your inner critic and simply write. You don't need to be J. K. Rowling or Gary Paulson to engage in modeled writing. Nancie Atwell's words (1998) should ease our minds: "You only have to write a little bit better than your students for them to take something away from your writing."

You are the expert writer in your classroom. *You* are the one to whom your students are looking for guidance, direction, and inspiration. They need *you* to come alongside them and show them how it's done. So close your classroom door if you must. Then write what's in your heart and on your mind.

Brick or Bulldozer

As I read the comments from the teachers I interviewed, I think there's a valuable lesson there for all of us who teach writing. Our words have enormous power. As shown, poor feedback can leave an indelible mark on a writer for years to come.

As I talk to students about their writing, I use a word picture to help me remember to choose my words carefully: I picture my words as either a *brick* or a *bulldozer*. The words I say, the feedback I give, can either build up a writer (brick) or tear him down (bulldozer).

I can imagine that most of us would like the words we choose to build up a writer's confidence and skill. If we want our words to be bricks, we need to use language that demonstrates respect. Remember: Sharing your writing with someone else puts you in an extremely vulnerable position. When our students write, they put their hearts and souls on the page, so it's important to treat each writer (and each piece of writing) with a light touch and a soft heart.

We build up writers when we say things like:

- *You have an interesting story to tell! I can't wait to see what you write next.*

- *Thank you for sharing your thinking and your writing with me.*

- *I'll show you something that has helped me as a writer. Would you like to give it a try? I'll help you.*

We tear down writers when we say things like:

- *Most of these words are misspelled. Go back and fix the spelling, and then bring it back to me to read.*

- *That's not writing. Start over.*

- *Most of your sentences are run-ons. Try again.*

The question then becomes: *What if a writer (or a part of his or her writing) needs attention or correction? How do you provide constructive feedback without allowing your words to become bulldozers?*

Here are some examples of how we can constructively and respectfully nudge writers when they need it.

Destructive Comments	Constructive Comments
Try writing that sentence again. It doesn't make any sense.	*As I reader, I couldn't tell if you were saying that Texas was hot or that the food you ate in Texas was hot. What can you do to help your reader?*
You don't have any periods here, so the sentence just goes on and on. You need to work on adding periods.	*Can I share a "writer's secret" with you? Can I show you what writers do when they want their reader to stop and take a breath? Writers add periods. The periods tell the reader where one sentence ends and another sentence begins.*
This is writing time, not drawing time. Stop drawing and add some writing to your page.	*Tell me about your picture. There's so much happening in your picture—it tells a story, doesn't it? Would you like to add some words so that your reader can know more about your story?*
This is so sloppy. I can't read it.	*Can you read me what you've written so far? Wow…you have a lot to say! Is this a piece of writing that you'd like to revise and edit so that it can be published, or is this a piece that is just for you?*

When you model your thinking and writing, your advice becomes more credible and your feedback has more value because you are doing the hard work of writing too.

Likewise, when we provide positive feedback, our comments need to be constructive, genuine, and *specific*. Vague comments, such as "Nice work!" simply aren't helpful.

Vague Feedback	Specific Feedback
Nice job.	*When I read this part, I can picture you wiggling that tooth back and forth! Your writing made me feel like I was right there!*
I like the diagram you added.	*I noticed that you added a diagram to teach your readers more about life in the desert. When I look at this diagram of a cactus that you included, I can see all the different parts. As a reader, that helps me know more.*
Great lead!	*Will you read your first three sentences aloud again? When I read those sentences, I want to keep reading! These sentences have made me curious and I want to know more. That's a smart thing to do when you are creating a lead. You want to make your reader want to keep reading. Always remember to do that when you are writing a lead.*

So, you might be wondering: *What do writing conferences and constructive feedback have to do with modeled writing?* In my own teaching, I found that one of the main benefits of modeled writing was that it forced me to engage in writing—with all of its struggles and triumphs—and this became enormously valuable when I gave feedback to student writers.

The atmosphere of the writing conference became more relaxed because I was simply one writer talking to another writer, rather than "The Teacher of Writing" swooping in to tell the students what was wrong with their pieces.

When you are engaging in modeled writing yourself, you are able to say things, such as: *I had a hard time coming up with the conclusion for my piece too. Would you like to hear what helped me?* Or: *One thing that helped make my piece more interesting was to speak directly to the reader. Can I show you how I did that?*

In other words, when you model your thinking and writing, your advice becomes more credible and your feedback has more value because you are doing the hard work of writing too. You, as the teacher, are seen as one writer in a community of writers and that helps guide and temper the feedback you provide.

A Little Writing Secret

Years ago, when I first began the practice of writing in front of my students every day, this is what it looked like: I asked students to meet me on the carpet and, using an easel and chart paper, I wrote. I smiled. I wrote. I smiled some more. What my students saw was a writer who was thoroughly enjoying the process of putting pen to paper. I showed confidence in my word choices. My countenance was bright. I was self-assured. I was unwavering. What my students didn't see were the hours and minutes leading up to that piece of writing. They didn't see me wracking my brain to choose an interesting topic. They didn't see or hear my first, second, or third attempts at a lead. They only saw the finished product of all of the internal thinking and processing I had done before the lesson.

This created a problem when my students left the carpet, returned to their seats, and began writing. When they met the inevitable challenges that all writers face, they had no idea how to handle them. I had allowed them to see me write, but I had neglected to give them an authentic view of writing.

I hadn't shown them what writers do when they get to a word they don't know how to spell. I hadn't demonstrated how writers sometimes stop to reread and then decide that what they've written so far is not at all what they had hoped to say. I hadn't cracked open my thinking and allowed them to see me trying to choose the descriptive words that would make my piece come alive for a reader. In truth, I was engaging in false advertising. The message I was giving my little cherubs was that writing was a breeze—a piece of cake! They had no idea that the writing process is sometimes messy and raw and beautiful and exhilarating and hard. I hadn't let them see me struggle.

A friend of mine is a writer by trade. One day, as we were discussing his latest book, I asked him if he enjoyed writing. He was quiet for a long moment and then finally said, "I enjoy having written." This makes perfect sense to me. There is nothing quite as satisfying as seeing a written work come to publication. The crisp pages, the pleasing layout, the weight of the book as you hold it in your hands. But the writing process itself? Well, sometimes that can be downright painful. Although the thoughts, ideas, and concepts can be vivid in our mind, the words to express them can often escape us.

Please don't misunderstand me—I'm not saying that everything about writing is arduous. There are moments when the words flow effortlessly and your fingers can't type fast enough to capture all of them. But there are just as many moments that are slow, tedious, and frankly, maddening.

So what is the writing process like for you? Do you enjoy writing? Does writing come easily? Or do you find it difficult? Let me put it this way: Are you happy to sit down at your computer to write report card comments, or would you rather have a root canal?

You're in good company if writing is difficult for you. William Zinsser, author of the classic book *On Writing Well*, says, "If you find that writing is hard, it's because it is hard. It's one of the hardest things that people do" (1976).

This, my friend, is the real world of writing, and I believe that we should let our students in on this little writing secret. Remember the concept of cognitive apprenticeship (Collins, Brown, Newman, 1989) that was discussed in Chapter 1? Cognitive apprenticeship invites us to externalize the processes that are usually carried out internally. In other words, students learn by watching someone else do something. So why wouldn't we let our students see the internal struggles and challenges that exist for all writers? If we allowed our students to watch another writer grapple with words, phrases, and ideas, it would give them an honest picture of what writing is all about and help them work through the inevitable obstacles that will be a part of their own writing experience. Don't be afraid to make the struggle visible to your students.

Educator and author Chris Lehman (2014) puts it this way, "When you write, really write, you appreciate more of the writers' blocks, confusions, and walls that arise for students. By writing yourself, you can show students points where you feel stuck as well as ways you worked through challenges."

So, what does this look like in practice? How can we think out loud as we wrestle with our own writing challenges? Here are a couple of examples of "teacher talk" that provide an honest peek into the process of writing.

I am thinking I want to start my narrative by describing the setting. That could really draw my reader in. Let's see, I could say, "The sun came up and there was a beautiful sunrise." Hmm… that's okay, but it's not very descriptive. My readers can't really see what I see. What else could I say? I could start with, "The first morning of June broke into a brilliant sunrise of yellows, pinks, and reds." I'm not happy with either one of those leads, but I'm just going to get one of them down on the page and then keep writing. After I've written a bit more, I'll come back and reread it. Maybe something better will come to me as I keep writing. Sometimes just getting more down on the page helps me when I'm stuck on a particular sentence.

I've been working on this paragraph for a while now, and it's still not working. I've included the facts about Rosa Parks' childhood, but it sounds dry, like an encyclopedia. I'm going to take a break from this section of my draft and come back to it. For now, I'm going to work on the timeline that I also want to include on this page. After taking a bit of break, I might have some fresh ideas about how to make that paragraph more interesting for my reader.

Writers, has this ever happened to you: You were writing and all of a sudden you came to a word that you didn't know how to spell? I'm sorry to be the bearer of bad news, but this is a problem that you will have for the rest of your life as a writer. We all think of words every now and then that we don't know how to spell. So let me show you some things that I do when I experience that writing challenge.

I've written the section of my travel brochure that tells about the national parks that people can see when they visit Montana, but I'm struggling with creating a sentence that will bring closure to this section. As it stands now, the section just ends—BAM! Sometimes, when I'm struggling with something like this, I look at published travel brochures to see how other writers conclude a particular section. Watch me as I look at a few brochures to see if there is an idea that might help me with this writing challenge.

What I'm trying to say is this: Don't let your own writing difficulties keep you from engaging in modeled writing. Wrestling with ideas and words is part of being a writer, and we do our students no favors when we pretend that we have it all together. Remember that you're modeling *process* and *decision-making*. And these things don't always come easily. When students see how we navigate our own writing jungles, they won't be caught off guard when they face their own.

So be transparent. Be real. Model your own thinking, reasoning, and problem-solving strategies. By doing so, you'll humanize writing and give your students the tools they need to be lifelong writers.

Chapter 4:
A FEW TIPS FOR SUCCESS (AND A LESSON LEARNED)

"When we develop a place where concepts
can be developed and patterns can be learned,
kids feel safe, take risks, and feel welcome in
every stage of the writing process."

— Jeff Anderson

Perhaps you are feeling motivated to give modeled writing its rightful place in your daily writing block. Perhaps you are anxious to jump in and begin making your own thinking and writing transparent for your students. If so, bravo!

Before you begin, allow me to share some tips that will help you as you unleash the power of modeled writing.

Create a Space for Learning

If you're going to gather your students for a modeled writing experience, it stands to reason that you'll need to provide space for them to gather. I have found that the power of teacher modeling diminishes when students are seated at their desks. Instead, I prefer to invite students to sit on the floor in close proximity to me. With learners close by, I can easily lean in, listen to partner conversations, and plan my next teaching move. This becomes much more difficult to do if students are at their desks and I'm at the front of the classroom. Gathering students together on the floor decreases the number of distractions as well. (Think of all of the items that can cause distraction in and around desks!)

Even fourth- and fifth-grade students can sit comfortably on the floor if they are provided with enough space. Tamara, a teacher of a 5/6 blend, told me that her students groaned a bit on the first day she called them to their class gathering place. But she stood firm and reassured her students that she would keep her mini-lessons brief and to the point so that they wouldn't find themselves on the carpet for long stretches of time. She stayed true to her word and it didn't take long for the students to acclimate. Now they gather comfortably (and even excitedly) on the floor several times a day for various reasons.

When teachers say, "My classroom feels cramped. I can't create a gathering space that's comfortable and has enough room for everyone," my response is: "Evaluate how you are using the space you have."

Some teachers have found that by utilizing a smaller teacher's desk (or by completely eliminating it), they can open up some much-needed space for students to gather, discuss, observe, and learn. Finding other options for the storage of teacher supplies that are not used on a daily basis can also help to free up space.

Other teachers have repurposed classroom areas in order to have a large gathering space. For example, one teacher I know created a classroom library that was the picture of organization and beauty. She placed book-lined shelves in the shape of the letter "U." Then she added a rug, a lamp for soft lighting, and a few plants. This large

and inviting space became the favorite hangout during independent reading and writing time. In addition, she repurposed the space by using it to gather her students for mini-lessons. She told them, "This is the perfect place for us to learn how to become better writers—we're surrounded by books written by so many fabulous authors!"

Once you have a gathering place designated, it's time to consider the materials you'll need in order to model your writing. I encourage teachers to use a low easel and chart paper so that everyone can see the writing. I prefer writing on chart paper rather than writing on a dry-erase board or an overhead projector for the simple reason that chart paper allows me to save my modeled writing and return to it again and again. If your classroom has an interactive whiteboard, it can be used for modeled writing as well. Whatever writing materials you choose to use, make sure that all students can easily see you and the piece of writing you are crafting.

Keep It Short and Sweet

While it's true that modeled writing can occur anytime during the instructional day, it is an integral part of the writing block. The writing block is the part of the day that provides students with explicit instruction and the time needed to practice writing.

A writing block consists of three basic parts:

1. A focused mini-lesson,

2. Independent writing time, and

3. Reflection.

The times listed below are general guidelines and may vary depending on the time of year and the writing stamina of the students in your classroom. For example, kindergarten teachers who are launching a writing block in September might begin with only five or 10 minutes of independent writing. Over time, as students' writing stamina increases, the independent writing time can be lengthened to as much as 30 minutes.

On the other hand, a fifth-grade teacher might be able to begin the year with 30–40 minutes of independent writing, especially if students have experienced sustained blocks of writing time in previous grades.

Component of a Writing Block	Time

Focused mini-lesson
    Teacher writes, explicitly teaches, and thinks aloud (models)
    Teacher sets the stage for writing
	8–10 minutes

Independent writing
    Students write
    Teacher coaches and confers with writers
	20–40 minutes, depending on the grade level and time of year

Reflection
Students and teacher gather to reflect:
  • *What did I learn about myself as I writer?*
  • *What new strategy did I try and how did it work?*
  • *How can I use what I learned to help me as a writer?*
	3–5 minutes

The truth is, when our *mini-lesson* becomes more of a *maxi-lesson,* we often lose the attention of our learners.

Modeled writing occurs during the mini-lesson portion of the writing block, and it's important to keep the modeling *brief*—no longer than 10 minutes or so. There are two main reasons for the brevity. The first reason has to do with attention span. Allow me to explain.

Years ago, I spent a day observing teachers in an elementary school in Melbourne, Australia. During lunch, I listened as one of the teachers reflected on a lesson she had taught earlier in the day. With a sigh, she told her colleague, "My lesson went much too long! The children were off with the fairies!"

Have you experienced a similar teaching moment? You're in the midst of a brilliant lesson. The stars have aligned, and you are *in the zone*. You are *teaching*. You are writing. You are invincible! Eventually, you come up for air and take a quick peek at your students. At that moment, it becomes abundantly clear that the students are with you physically, but they are no longer *with you*. Dylan has tied his shoelaces together and is now using his teeth to try to loosen the knot. Olivia is braiding the hair of the girl in front of her and whispering, *"Hold still!"* Zach has discovered a bit of an abandoned crayon on the floor and is attempting to write his name on a corner of the carpet. Your students are…well… *off with the fairies*. The truth is, when our *mini-lesson* becomes more of a *maxi-lesson*, we often lose the attention of our learners.

I've heard it said that, in general, the average age of the students in front of you is roughly equal to how many minutes they can sustain attention. If that's true, then it means that most second graders can attend to "teacher talk" for roughly 7.5 minutes. Likewise, fifth graders can sustain attention for about 10.5 minutes.

So, you might be wondering: Should the mini-lesson only last 5.5 minutes for kindergarten? Many teachers find that kindergartners can attend to a 10-minute mini-lesson as long as there are opportunities for partner talk within the 10 minutes. For example, a kindergarten teacher might explicitly model for five minutes, ask partners to talk about what they noticed, and then continue modeling for an additional three or four minutes, if needed.

You might imagine then, that when I present workshops to teachers, I can present information and content for 30 minutes or more before providing time for teachers to process. That isn't the case. In fact, I've found that more deep learning happens when I follow a "10:2 rule." I try to talk *at* teachers for no longer than 10 minutes. Then I give participants two minutes to turn and talk so that they can process what they've just heard. I could just ramble on for quite a while, but from experience, I know that teachers won't be able to hear what I have to say next because their brains will still be thinking about and processing what I've just said. The two-minute talk time allows them to "chew" on what they just heard, reflect on their own teaching, and listen to the thoughts of others.

The second reason for keeping your modeled writing short and sweet has to do with priorities. When we keep our modeling and "teacher talk" brief, we protect the most important time period in the writing block— the time that students have to independently write.

Think about it. There is a reason airline pilots spend a lot of time in the cockpit before they receive their license. They don't spend hours and hours sitting and listening to someone else *talk* about flying. They get their backsides in a cockpit, and they practice flying. Skiers become better skiers by skiing. Swimmers have to don a swimsuit and spend some time in the water. Readers become better readers by reading. And writers become better writers by actually *writing*. To become fluent and proficient writers, our students need large chunks of time to engage with pen and paper. To do that, we must ensure that our modeling is brief.

Do you find it difficult to keep your mini-lessons mini? Do your modeled writing experiences tend to go on and on? If so, let me assure you that you are not alone. Almost every teacher I know has difficulty with this (including the author of this book).

For years, I struggled to keep my modeling brief. As hard as I tried, my mini-lessons always went longer than I had hoped. Day after day, I ended up shortening the time my students had to actually *write*. One day, at my wit's end, I asked a colleague for help. She suggested that I purchase a kitchen timer and simply set the timer for eight or 10 minutes before beginning my lesson. It was extremely difficult at first, but mindful of the ticking timer, I noticed that, over time, my teaching became more crisp and clear. It was then that I realized something: The key to making my modeling brief was staring at me the whole time—I needed to limit the focus.

Limit the Focus

It's important to remember that modeled writing is not an invitation to teach the world of writing. We can unleash the power of modeling only when we choose *one teaching focus* and explicitly model *it*—and nothing more.

In order to illustrate this, let's examine two different modeled writing experiences from a primary classroom:

> *Writers, today I want to show you something authors do to make their writing easier for a reader to read. Writers leave spaces between their words! When a writer leaves a space between each word, the reader can tell where one word ends and another word begins. Okay, I am going to write about how the butterfly comes out of the chrysalis. I think I'll say, "The butterfly swallows air and gets bigger. The chrysalis bursts open so the butterfly can pull itself out." The first word I'll write is "The." Now, because this is the first word of my sentence, I need a capital letter, don't I? Watch me write the capital letter "T." The rest of the letters in that word will be lowercase. I just need to make the first letter a capital because it's the beginning of my sentence. Okay, how do I spell "The"? Oh! That word is on our word wall, so I'm going to use the word wall to help me spell that word.*

This well-meaning teacher started off strong. She explained *exactly* what she wanted to teach her young writers—how writers leave spaces between words to help their readers. However, once she started writing, she soon lost focus. In her modeling, she inadvertently included two additional focus points—starting sentences with capital letters and using the word wall to spell unknown words. Both of these focus points are important things to teach emergent writers, but she didn't remain true to the focus of her modeled writing. She got off track.

Now, let's take a look at another modeled writing experience:

Today I want to show you something writers do to make their writing easier for a reader to read. Writers leave spaces between their words! When a writer leaves a space between each word, the reader can tell where one word ends and another word begins. I think I'll say, "The butterfly swallows air and gets bigger. The chrysalis bursts open so the butterfly can pull itself out." I've got so many words that I want to write! Watch what I do each time I write a word. Okay, the first word is "The." Now that I've written that word, I'm going to put my finger here after the word. This helps me to remember that I need to leave a space about as wide as my finger between each of my words. Now I'll write the next word, "butterfly." Now that I've written another word, I'm going to leave a space. Okay, the next word I want to write is "swallows." Watch how, this time, I leave a space between "butterfly" and "swallows." That way, my reader will know that one word is ending and another word is beginning. That will really help my reader!

(After writing a sentence or two) Writers, today I showed you how I leave a space between my words to help my reader know where one word ends and another word begins. Leaving spaces between words helps others read what I've written. Today, as you write, try using a finger space between your words, and see what you think. Who thinks they are ready to try that?

This teacher might have been tempted to remind her students about capitals, spelling, and word choice. In fact, she may have been tempted to talk a little bit about those fascinating butterflies, but she stayed focused on her *one* teaching point—word spacing—and, as a result, her modeled writing remained brief and focused.

Limiting the focus of our teaching is a lot like using a small nozzle on a large hose. Imagine you have a hose with a large nozzle. If you were to turn on the faucet, the water would come out of the nozzle, but the water might only spray one or two feet in front of you. Now imagine the same hose with a much smaller nozzle. If you turned on the hose, the same volume of water would shoot through the nozzle, but the water would travel much, much further. You might be able to spray water on the flowers clear on the other side of your yard! Limiting the focus of our teaching is like using that smaller nozzle on our hose. In other words, if my modeling has a laser-like focus, it allows my students to engage in much deeper learning. In contrast, if I try to accomplish too much in my modeled writing, the depth of learning simply isn't there.

Catch and Release

While it's true that students need to see what you do as you craft a piece of writing, that doesn't mean that you need to write an entire piece in one sitting. Sometimes, it's just as powerful to craft a few sentences or a single paragraph and then allow students to try out the skill on their own. I call this "catch and release." We "catch" our students' attention with a brief and focused mini-lesson and then "release" them to try it out!

Tamara, a teacher of a 5/6 blend, did just that when she showed her students how to craft a lead for a book review. They had been examining published book reviews for a few days, and Tamara was ready to think out loud as she wrote the lead for her own book review.

She began by saying: *One of my favorite books is* In a Sunburned Country *by Bill Bryson. I laughed out loud when I read it—all of his travel adventures are so entertaining and funny! But this book wasn't only funny. It was also filled with lots of interesting facts about Australia. I learned so much!*

I'm ready to write the review of this book, and I want my first few sentences to catch the attention of my readers and make them want to read this book too. Let's see. The book is funny and interesting, but it's also factual. So I think I'll start by saying: If you enjoy interesting, educational, and hilarious books about travel, In a Sunburned Country *should be on your shelf!"*

Modeled writing

If you enjoy interesting, educational, and hilarious books about travel, *In a Sunburned Country* should be on your shelf! In this book, Bill Bryson takes us along on his wild journey throughout Australia, where he encounters his fair share of adventure."

After she modeled, Tamara's students briefly chatted with a partner about the book they were going to review and their ideas for an inviting lead. Then she released them to write.

Here is the dynamic lead that her student, Max, crafted when reviewing *Rifles for Watie* by Harold Keith:

> If you take pleasure in captivating, stimulating, and bloodcurdling novels, *Rifles for Watie* should definitely be on your "must read list." In this book, Jefferson Davis Bussey, a boy named after the confederate president, joins the Union Army.

It was after this experience that Tamara told me, "I just model a little and then send them off to write. I'm always surprised and amazed by what my students can do when I get out of the way."

For larger writing tasks or skills that require more explicit teaching and modeling, you might consider breaking up the mini-lesson. Model a bit of the writing task, send students off to try it, and then bring them back together for additional modeling. In other words, it's sometimes a good idea to break the modeling into "bite-sized" pieces so that students don't become overwhelmed with too much information at once.

In Tamara's classroom, she might give her students a chance to get started with their book reviews. Then she might call them back together so that she can think out loud and demonstrate how she crafts a satisfying ending for her book review.

> "I just model a little and then send them off to write. I'm always surprised and amazed by what my students can do when I get out of the way."

Encourage Talk

Pamela A. Mason and Emily Phillips Galloway, in an article written for *Reading Today* in 2012, made a bold statement when they said, "If there is *one instructional strategy* that teachers can implement to support the academic success of children, especially those in low socioeconomic communities, it is to let them talk" (emphasis mine). Simply put, when students engage in peer conversations centered on literacy (reading and writing), powerful learning can take place. Researchers Applebee, Langer, Nystrand, and Gamoran (2003) found that "when students' classroom experiences emphasize high academic demands and discussion-based approaches to the development of understanding, students internalize the knowledge and skills necessary to engage in challenging literacy tasks on their own." Douglas Fisher, Nancy Frey, and Carol Rothenberg, in their book *Content-Area Conversations* (2008), put it this way: "Oral language is the foundation of literacy, and as such, it requires focused attention in planning."

Instead of shutting out talk in our classroom, we should be embracing it—even during modeled writing.

So if I may simplify things, the research is saying that your students need to talk more. Yes, you read that sentence accurately—I said "more." Instead of shutting out talk in our classroom, we should be embracing it—even during modeled writing. Allow me to explain: While it's true that modeled writing is an opportunity for the teacher to do the majority of the thinking, writing, and speaking, there should still be frequent opportunities for students to think, wonder, and *talk*.

During modeled writing, I find it valuable to invite students to share their thinking with a partner. For example, if I'm teaching students how to choose words that evoke strong sensory images for the reader, I might say: *Think for a moment. Why would it be important for writers to create sensory images for their reader? Share your ideas with your partner.* Or if I'm showing students how I decide where to start a new paragraph in my writing, I might ask: *Partners, what did you notice me doing that you could do?* If I come to a particularly tricky word when I'm writing, I might say: *What did I do when I got to a word I didn't know how to spell? Tell your partner what you noticed.*

However, I would caution you about asking for and accepting suggestions from students as you write. If you ask students to provide ideas for your writing, the writing experience is no longer modeled writing. It becomes *shared* writing. (See page 16 in Chapter 1.) Furthermore, each time you call on a student, you inevitably lose focus and the attention of the rest of the students.

So instead of eliciting help and ideas from your students, let them know that this is a time for you to show them your thinking and writing.

Teacher tips for partner talk:

- Consider identifying partners before they come to the gathering place for modeled writing. This saves valuable time because students won't be scrambling to find a partner each time you ask them to discuss something.

- To encourage eye contact, teach partners to turn "knee-to-knee and eye-to-eye" when they are talking.

- Give students a few moments to think quietly before they turn and talk.

- Keep the talking times brief. A 30-second to one-minute partner talk is usually sufficient.

- Listen in while partners are talking. Partner conversations give you valuable information! By listening, you can assess students' thinking and learning. This helps you plan your next teaching move.

- Decide on a signal that will let partners know when it's time to wrap up their discussion and bring their focus back to you.

- At times, when students finish their discussions, you might want to take a moment to highlight a few things you heard as you listened in. You might say: *I heard some partnerships say* _____. *Others of you said* _____.

When we provide opportunities to think, talk, and wonder, we invite learners to become active participants in their own learning and we send the clear message that, in this classroom, we are a community of learners.

Teachers often ask me: "What do you do when students won't talk or they don't know what to say?" My response is generally this: "If you expect it, teach it. If you teach it, model it." Some of your students will undoubtedly need a bit more support and scaffolding in order to fully engage in academic conversations about writing (and other content areas).

> As with any other skill, academic discourse needs to be explicitly taught.

As with any other skill, academic discourse needs to be explicitly taught. At the beginning of the year, I ask a colleague to come into my classroom so that I can *show* my students what partner talk looks like and sounds like. I model!

Every day that we are together this year, I will invite you to talk with a partner about what you are noticing, thinking, and wondering. So today, I want to show you what it looks like and sounds like when two people are having a conversation about learning. Ms. Dunkin is going to help me. First, when Ms. Dunkin and I begin talking, we turn our bodies so that we are facing each other. In other words, we sit "eye-to-eye and knee-to-knee." When we engage in partner talk in our classroom, I'll usually give you something to think about and discuss. For example, I might say, "Tell your partner what you do as a writer when you try to spell a tricky word." Let's imagine that the teacher just asked that question of us. Watch how Ms. Dunkin and I think for a moment before we begin talking. We are thinking about what we do as writers. After we've thought for a moment, we start talking. We aren't going to talk at the same time—we're going to take turns like you do when you are playing "catch" with a ball. Watch and listen as we have a conversation, and notice what we do.

Some teachers have found that creating and posting a list of conversation starters, like the ones below, helps those students who might need a nudge to get started. If you decide to use a list like this, be sure to *model* how you and your partner use the list to help you converse.

Conversation starters that support active discussion:

- *I'm thinking…*
- *I wonder…*
- *I'm not sure. What do you think?*
- *I noticed…*
- *That's a good point. I'm also thinking…*
- *What if…*
- *I have an idea…*
- *I learned…*
- *I understand what you're saying, but I think…*
- *I was confused when…*
- *I agree/disagree with _____ because _____…*
- *What you said made me think about…*
- *In my opinion…*
- *I have something to add to what _____ said…*
- *I used to think _____ , but now I think _____…*
- *I'm realizing…*
- *On the other hand…*

In short, don't give up when it comes to incorporating more student conversation during the modeled writing experiences. Quality conversation, like any other skill, takes time, practice, and patience.

Make Your Thinking Transparent

Thinking aloud is one of the cornerstone characteristics of modeling that sets it apart from other kinds of writing instruction. If we don't make our thinking visible for our students, they are simply watching our pen move over paper. There's no power. The transformational impact of modeling exists in the think-aloud language that we use.

Many teachers have noticed that students will often mimic the language of the teacher in their own conversations about writing.

When we make our own thinking transparent, students begin to develop a language to talk about writing. In fact, many teachers have noticed that students will often mimic the language of the teacher in their own conversations about writing.

When I engage in modeled writing, I like to make it very clear to students what I am doing and why I am doing it. I often say something like: *I'm going to be thinking aloud as I write because I want to show you how writers think. When I'm thinking out loud, your job is to **listen** and **observe**. Notice what I do as a writer.*

Below are some sentence starters that I use when thinking out loud:

- *I'm thinking…*
- *Watch me as I…*
- *I'm wondering…*
- *As I reread this, I'm thinking…*
- *Notice how I…*
- *Watch what I do as a writer when I…*
- *Notice the way that I…*
- *Look closely as I…*

After I have thought out loud and have written a sentence or two, I often invite students to reflect on what they just observed. For example, I might say: *Did you see how I did that? Did you see how I spoke directly to my reader in this section? Did you see how I used the word "you" as I tried to draw my reader into the setting?*

When you model, remember to make your thinking transparent. It's imperative that our students see how writing begins in the writer's mind and ends up on the paper.

Determine If the Model Is a Tool or a Mandate

Teachers often ask me, "If you model something, does that mean that all students *have* to try the skill that was modeled?" The answer is sometimes "yes" and sometimes "no."

There may be times when you'd like everyone to try something you've modeled. For example, if you're showing students how writers sometimes use sketches to organize their narratives, you might say:

Today, I showed you how I make three little sketches that help me remember what happened first, next, and last. I showed you how I can use those sketches to help me create a piece of writing that's organized and easy for my reader to follow. Today, I'd like all of us to try this strategy and see what we think. When independent writing time is over, let's gather back together so we can talk about how it helped us (or didn't help us) as writers.

It's imperative that students have a chance to reflect on the skill or strategy and decide if it was helpful or not. When students gather again after independent writing time, you might say: *What did you think about using sketches to plan out your writing? Did they help you as a writer or not? Why? Do you think they improved your piece of writing?*

Other times, the skill you model may simply be another tool in your students' "writer's toolbox," but not something that all students *must* try. In other words, we may invite students to try it, but we don't necessarily *mandate* that students try it.

For example, if I demonstrate how I include onomatopoeia in my personal narrative so that my writing has a little pizazz, I might invite students to try it out but not require that all students include onomatopoeia. I could say: *Adding some onomatopoeia—words that sound like the sound they represent—made this sentence much more interesting. As you work on your narratives today, you might think about adding some onomatopoeia to your writing and see how you like it. It's just one more tool you can put in your writer's toolbox.*

Tell Students Why

Years ago, I was asked to visit several classrooms and talk to students about their writing. When I came into one classroom, I noticed that the students were busily working on creating a glossary for a piece of informational writing they had done. When I asked students why they were creating a glossary, they replied with "Our teacher told us to" and "We learn how to make a glossary in third grade." It was clear that they had no real understanding of why they were creating a glossary. The teacher was probably clear about her purpose: She wanted her writers (and readers) to understand that glossaries provide definitions to domain-specific words that appear in text. However, she never told her students that.

Students need to know the value and purpose of what they are being asked to do. So once you model your own thinking and writing and you invite them to try the new skill in their own writing, make sure you check for understanding. You might ask: *Why are we doing this? Why is this important?* In other words, be explicit about *why* you are teaching what you are teaching.

Lessons Learned

Chris was a student in my first-grade classroom. He had dark brown hair and eyes that were bright and curious. Chris was always on the move. He was one of those active and endearing boys that make our job fun and unexpected.

One morning, early in the school year, I taught a mini-lesson on how writers think about a topic, draw a picture to help them think more deeply about it, and then write about it. I carefully modeled how to designate space on the paper for the picture and another space for the writing. I thought out loud as I used a pencil to sketch my thinking and then added some words. It wasn't a perfect lesson, but it was solid. I had kept my modeling brief and focused, made my thinking transparent, and invited students to talk with a partner about what they noticed me do as a writer.

Once I released my students to write, I began roaming the classroom so that I could coach and confer. Most students were dutifully designating spaces for their picture and spaces for their writing. Students were chatting, and there was a productive hum in the classroom.

As I sidled next to Chris, I noticed something was amiss. Chris had used a black fat-tipped marker and, starting at the top of the page and moving his marker side to side, had filled in most of his page with black. There was approximately one inch of blank space at the bottom of the page, but the rest of the page was completely…black.

To be honest, my first reaction was irritation. Didn't he hear any of my brilliant mini-lesson? Fighting my feelings of frustration, I considered what I should say to Chris. After a few moments, I finally settled on a "go-to" sentence that all good teachers of writing use: *Tell me about your piece.* Chris looked up at me and simply said, "It's dirt."

Can I be honest? What I wanted to say was: *Chris, today I asked you to designate a space for your picture and a space for your words. I asked you to use pencil. Please get a new piece of paper and start again.* Instead, I knelt down next to Chris and quietly said: *You know, as a reader, I had a hard time telling that was dirt. What can you do to help your reader?*

Chris thought for a moment and then replied, "I could add some words!" I watched as Chris added "drt" to the only white space left on the page. Then he used brown and green markers to add worms, plants, and roots to the black "dirt" on his page. I exclaimed: *Ah! The details you added to your picture and the word you added at the bottom really helped me as a reader! Always remember that, Chris. Details and words help your reader know more about your writing.*

As I reflect on this experience, I think there are a couple of lessons from which we all might benefit.

The first lesson is this: Not all modeling sticks. Regie Routman (2005) said, "Don't assume that because you have modeled writing, your students 'got' your demonstration. Good teaching is more difficult than that." She speaks the truth. You may model something perfectly, but some writers will not be ready or willing to try it out—yet. Resist the urge to be discouraged or frustrated. Keep modeling. Rome wasn't built in a day. Children don't learn to read in an afternoon. Pilots don't fly a 747 across the Atlantic after two flying lessons. Keep modeling, keep demonstrating, keep encouraging, and trust the process.

The second lesson is this: Relationships trump compliance. We must remember that we are teaching writers, not fixing pieces of writing. The piece of writing will fade in time, but the writer lives on. If I had chastised Chris for not following directions, I might have achieved compliance, but I may have damaged the relationship between Chris and me. The relationship between teacher and student—between one writer and another—is paramount. Our relationship (and Chris's writing) was salvaged that day. I was able to provide some focused instruction for Chris, and he was able to consider his writing—and his reader—with a fresh insight. So fight the urge to be frustrated that your students don't "get" your lesson. Rather, consider each child as a unique writer in process. Then offer a word of encouragement to help each child take the next step.

> Relationships trump compliance. We must remember that we are teaching writers, not fixing pieces of writing. The piece of writing will fade in time, but the writer lives on.

Chapter 5:

WHAT SKILLS SHOULD I MODEL?

"Be authentic with what you teach. Kids must internalize the reason for using descriptive words, strong verbs, leads—otherwise these lessons become writing exercises in isolation. Think about the purpose of a lesson."

— Regie Routman

Teachers often ask me if there is a list of skills and writing tools that I use to guide my teaching and modeled writing. While there is no magic list of writing skills that should be modeled, there are a few considerations when choosing a focus for your modeled writing.

Base Some Modeling on What You See in Student Writing

First and foremost, what you choose to model should come from what you see your students doing as writers. This means that while your students are independently writing, you are not at your desk checking e-mail. You are walking around the classroom. You are leaning in and listening to children. You are engaging in conversations with students about their writing. You are coaching. You are conferring. And you are engaging in assessment.

Now, dear reader, please don't tune out when you read the word "assessment." In the last decade or so, the word "assessment" has been hijacked. It has come to mean a plethora of things in education, and some teachers start to feel a bit queasy when they encounter it. In the minds of many (including students, parents, and community members), assessment means a high-stakes test or an evaluative judgment of a student's work. While assessment can mean those things—assessment *of* learning—there is also a place for a different kind of assessment—assessment *for* learning (Stiggins, 2004). This kind of ongoing, formative assessment provides valuable information about students and guides teachers as they make instructional decisions.

In my mind, it helps to boil writing assessment down to two questions: *What is this writer doing **well**, and what might be the **next step** for this writer?* To be sure, assessment can be much more complicated than that, but when all is said and done, doesn't it all come down to these two questions? When I focus on those two things—what the student is doing well and what the student needs next—it simplifies my thinking and, in turn, simplifies my teaching.

Allow me to illustrate by examining the following student samples:
GRADE 1

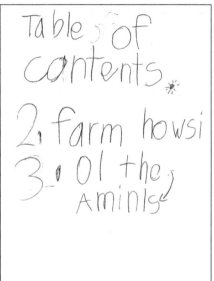

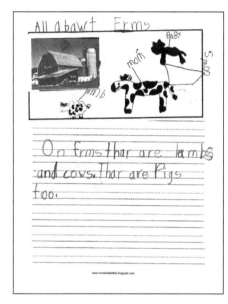

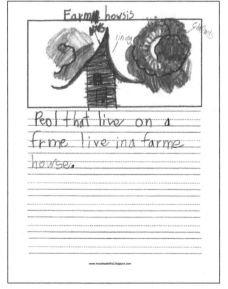

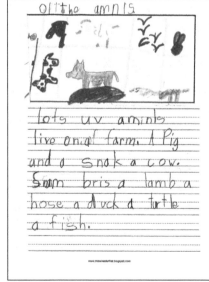

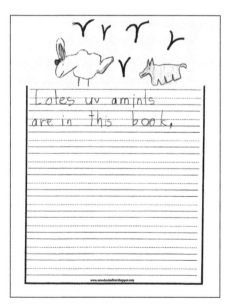

What is this writer doing well?

- The writer has included a table of contents to help her reader navigate the piece.

- She's added photographs, illustrations, and diagrams that add interest and clarity.

- She's included spaces between her words and her spelling is readable.

What are some next steps for this writer?

- She's given the reader some facts about farms, but she could add more details. For example, as a reader, I want to know more about the people who live on a farm. What do they do? How do they care for all of the animals on the farm? What special equipment do they use?

- This writer could benefit from learning how to craft a satisfying ending. How could we wrap up a piece about farms? What have other authors done when ending their pieces?

- Like most emergent writers, she jumps right in with facts about farms. Perhaps this writer is ready to learn how to introduce the reader to the topic *before* giving facts about the topic.

GRADE 4

No More Homework

I think teachers should not give students homework. It takes up too much time. It also is not helpful for students.

One reason students should not have homework is it takes up too much time. Also children's teachers give too much homework and students don't get to enjoy the outdoors. Students also don't get to have social time with their friends. Teachers give EXTRA homework and it's sometimes not helpful. Some students think homework is boring.

Another reason students should not have homework is it not helpful. Also some students don't understand the work the teachers give them. Parents try to show children different ways to do their homework but it makes students confused. Also the United States has the lowest test scores because of too much homework. Homework also makes students stress and makes them not want to do it.

In conclusion students should not have homework. It takes up too much time. It also isn't helpful. Students should leave the homework alone and enjoy the outdoors!

By: Montanna

What is this writer doing well?

- The writer has clearly articulated an opinion and has provided several reasons to support that opinion.

- She shows a beginning understanding of paragraphing.

- There is an organizational structure to the piece, and she has utilized linking words to help the reader move from one paragraph to the next (e.g., "one reason," "another reason," "in conclusion").

What are some next steps for this writer?

- This student might benefit from modeling that shows how to craft a topic sentence and supporting details. There's a topic sentence in the second paragraph, but the writer gets off track and begins to include other reasons to support her opinion rather than details that support the main topic of the paragraph.

- She could use support in crafting a lead that is enticing and draws the reader in.

- Instruction on how to examine and vary the sentence beginnings would help this writer.

- She could also learn how to use a variety of sentence lengths to add interest and fluency.

As you can see, there's a great deal of "assessment data" that I can gather about these students by simply examining their writing pieces. On pages 140 and 141 in the Appendix, you'll find samples of the record sheets I use when I confer with students.

However, assessment is only useful if it informs my instruction. Therefore, any information I gather while conferring with a writer will only truly be useful if I use that information to inform my next teaching move. I wouldn't recommend addressing *all* of the skills that child needs in one conference, but I can definitely focus on and teach *one* of the skills. However, if I notice that many of the writers in my classroom are experiencing similar writing challenges, I can and should teach that skill as a mini-lesson and *model*.

For example, if I notice that many of the writers in my kindergarten class are using mostly pictures to convey their thoughts and ideas, I might model how I label my pictures to help my reader know more about my topic, therefore encouraging my writers to include more letters and words when writing.

I could say: *Yesterday, I saw a mother duck and three ducklings cross the street right in front of my car! Watch me as I write about it today. First, I'll draw a picture of what I saw. Now I'm going to add some words to tell my reader even more. I am going to add a label. This duck is the mother, so I'll make a line from her out here to the empty space on my page so I can write the words "mother duck." When I write some letters and words, it will let my reader know more about my picture and about my story.*

Likewise, if I observe that many of my fifth-grade writers are beginning every sentence of their personal narratives with the word "I," I might let them listen in as I think out loud about varying the sentence beginnings in my narrative.

I might say: *We've been working on our personal narratives, and you are all off to a great start! One of the challenges of writing a personal narrative (and any piece of writing, for that matter) is to keep your sentence beginnings varied. Watch me as I work on this paragraph in my narrative. I want the first sentence to be: "I looked around and realized that nothing looked familiar." For my next sentence, I want to say: "I was lost and I knew it." Hmm…I just used the word "I" to begin the first sentence, so I'm not sure I want to use it again. Using different sentence beginnings makes my writing more interesting. I think I'll change the first sentence so that it doesn't begin with "I." I could say: "Looking around, I realized that nothing looked familiar." Let's see how that sounds. "Looking around, I realized that nothing looked familiar. I was lost and I knew it." I think that works better. Don't you?*

My general rule of thumb is this: If 40–50 percent of my writers are experiencing challenges with the same skill, I teach that skill in a modeled writing experience. On the other hand, if only one or two students need work on a particular skill, I might simply address it during an individual conference.

The bottom line is this: Notice what your writers are doing well. Tune in and listen to them as they talk about their writing. Pay attention to what's causing them difficulty too, and then base some of your modeling on the challenges they are facing. In that way, your assessment will become an integral part of your teaching, which is the way it was meant to be.

Skills That All Writers Need

In addition to teaching skills that the writers in your classroom need, there are some skills that can benefit all writers. These skills are part of becoming a lifelong writer.

Often, at the end of a modeled writing experience, I ask students: *Why do you think I showed you this? Why do you think I taught you this writing skill?* It's always interesting (and sometimes entertaining) to hear the responses. For example, sometimes I hear students say: *You taught us this so that we would be smarter!* After they've had a chance to think and talk, I usually say: *I taught you this because this is something you can use every day as a writer!*

I ask these questions purposefully. Throughout the modeled writing experience, I want students to be in a constant state of wonder, thinking, "How can I use this? How will this impact my life as a writer?"

These questions also serve as an internal check for me. When planning my modeled writing focus, I should be asking myself, *Why am I teaching my students this? Is this something that will help them today and every day?* The truth is, if I don't truly value the skill that I am teaching, if I don't think that my students will need this skill to become more accomplished and invested writers, then I need to think twice before teaching it.

In addition, when I'm choosing a focus skill to model, I ask myself three essential questions:

1. Is this *meaningful?*

2. Is this *purposeful?*

3. Will this *enhance* the writing that my students do?

If I can answer "yes" to these questions, I feel comfortable to move forward with the lesson.

While this is not an exhaustive list, here are several skills that I think are valuable to all writers, along with the "teacher talk" that could be used when you model them. Starting on page 90, you'll find several full-length sample lessons and models.

Writing with the reader in mind

- *I think I'll add more details to this section of my narrative. I want my readers to feel as though they are right there with me, standing next to the huge waterfall. The waterfall was so loud! I couldn't hear anything but the rushing water. So I think I'll write, "The deafening sound of the rushing water drowned out all other noises, so I didn't even try to speak." I remember that I could feel the cool mist coming off the waterfall, so I think I'll add something about that next.*

Modeled Writing

The deafening sound of the rushing water drowned out all other noises, so I didn't even try to speak. Instead, I gazed up at the rock face to where the waterfall started, letting the cool mist surround me and cool my tired and aching body.

Revising with the reader in mind

- *I'm worried that this section isn't clear, and I think my reader may be confused. I'm going to rework this part and see if I can improve the organization. Watch me as I do that.*

- *My sentences don't seem to flow when I read this piece aloud. I think I need to vary my sentence lengths to make it more pleasant for my reader to read.*

Modeled Writing: Before Revision

I think children should go to bed early. They do a lot during the day. They need rest. If they rest, they will have more energy. The rest will recharge them.

Modeled Writing: After Revision

"It's time for bed!" For most children, these words bring groans. Even though most children would prefer to stay up late, I think an early bedtime is essential. Children are constantly moving throughout the day—running, playing, thinking, reading, and writing—and all of this activity requires a lot of energy. It stands to reason that a child needs a lot of rest to be recharged and re-energized for the next day.

Editing with the reader in mind

- *Our writing conventions matter. When my spelling, capitalization, and punctuation are correct, it helps my reader focus in on my piece. If those things aren't correct, my reader will be distracted by all of the mistakes and won't be able to tune in to my message. I'm going to edit because I respect my reader.*

Stopping often to reread

- *I've written a few sentences, and now I'm going to stop and reread what I've written so far. I want to hear how it sounds and see if there's anything I want to change.*

Determining the audience and purpose and then choosing a structure that supports the purpose

- *Last night, I went for a bike ride, and I noticed a lot of trash left behind at our neighborhood park. To be honest, I was a bit irritated, but then I thought, "I should write about this!" I'm thinking I could create and display a poster encouraging people to put their trash in the trash can when they visit the park.*

- *I could simply write a narrative that tells how much I love Glacier National Park. Or I could create a travel brochure about the park. Perhaps the visitor's center would be willing to display my work when I'm finished.*

Living in a constant state of composition (thinking about your writing even when you're not writing)

- *When I was grocery shopping last night, I chose an apple from the pile of apples in the produce section and, when I did, dozens of apples came crashing down to the floor. Everyone in that part of the store stopped and stared at me. At first, I was embarrassed, but then I started laughing. Other shoppers came to help me clean up the mess. As we were picking up apples from the floor, I thought to myself, "I should write about this!" Writers do that: They think about their writing even when they're not writing.*

- *You know, I've been working on this section about the events that led up to the Civil War. Well, as I was driving to school this morning, a great idea came to me! That happens to me sometimes.*

Spelling consciousness (noticing when words don't look quite right)

- *The word "asparagus" doesn't look right to me. I don't want to stop writing because I'm not sure how to spell this word; but I do want to remember to come back to it and figure out the correct spelling. I think I'll circle this word for now and then come back to it later.*

Using writing to help you reflect, plan, or learn

- *I have three things I need to pack for our field trip tomorrow. I'm going to use this sticky note and write them down in a list. Sometimes writing things down helps me to remember.*

- *I just read this paragraph about the respiratory system. I'm going to jot down a few notes to help me remember what I learned.*

Adjusting voice and tone to match the audience

- *I'm writing this letter to our town's mayor, so I want the tone to be respectful and formal. I need to show respect for his position.*

- *This poster is going to be placed in the kindergarten wing of our school, so I need my writing and visuals to be clear and easy for young readers to understand.*

Using mentor texts to improve writing

- *I noticed that the author of this book added photographs and captions to some of the pages. It makes the book more interesting. I think I'll add some photographs and captions to my writing too.*

- *Listen to how Elizabeth Raum, the author of the book* Costa Rica, *started her book: "Have you ever been to Costa Rica?" She speaks right to us, the readers, and she makes us feel as though we are actually in Costa Rica. I want to try something similar in my piece about the Amazon.*

Skills That Support Specific Text Types

There will be times when you invite the writers in your classroom to explore different text types and genres. During these times, you'll undoubtedly want to model some of the skills necessary to be successful with a particular text type.

Again, my goal is not to create an exhaustive list, but here are a few key skills to model when your students are crafting informative, opinion, or narrative pieces.

In the Appendix, starting on page 124, you'll find samples of planning templates that I use when planning to study a particular writing genre.

Informative/explanatory writing

- Researching

  - *I need to find more information about why wolves howl. I found a few great nonfiction books about wolves. Watch me as I use the index and the table of contents to help me find the information I need.*

  - *I found an article about tornadoes that I think I can use to collect some information for my report. Watch me as I jot down some key words and phrases in my research journal.*

- Using multiple sources

  - *This book about grizzly bears gave me a lot of information, but when I'm writing an informative piece, I want to make sure I gather facts from more than one author. I'm going to use this book, but I'm also going to use these other books and articles to help me gather information too.*

- Using reliable sources

  - *I found some books that I can use to research sharks, and now I need to think about each one and decide whether it will give me credible and reliable information. As I read the inside back cover of Surprising Sharks by Nicola Davies, I noticed that Nicola Davies is a zoologist. That suggests that her work is well researched and credible.*

- Citing sources

  - *I've been using several different books, articles, and websites to find out more about Harriet Tubman, and I need to cite those books for my reader. When I make a list of sources that I used, it lets my reader know where I gathered my information, and it gives them ideas of where to go to find out more about Harriet Tubman. Watch me as I list the title and author for each book I used.*

Modeled Writing

Sources:

A Picture Book of Harriet Tubman by David A. Adler

Go Free or Die: A Story about Harriet Tubman by Jeri Chase Ferris

Harriet Tubman: Conductor on the Underground Railroad by Ann Petry

Moses: When Harriet Tubman Led Her People to Freedom
by Carole Boston Weatherford

- Turning research notes into running text

  - *I've collected some fascinating facts about how to stay safe during a tornado in my research journal. When I collected them, I simply jotted down words or phrases. Now I'm going to take those words and phrases and turn them into sentences for my piece. In my notes, I see that I wrote "underground shelter" because I read that if a tornado is approaching, you should stop whatever you are doing and head to an underground shelter. I think I'll write, "At the first sign of a tornado, it's important to stop whatever you are doing and find a safe shelter. If your house has an underground shelter, go there quickly. These rooms are the safest places to be during a tornado." Did you see how I used the words "underground shelter" from my research journal to create these sentences? The next word I jotted down was "basement" because when I researched tornadoes, I found out that if you don't have an underground shelter nearby, you can go into the basement of a building. So, next, I think I'll write, "If you don't have access to an underground tornado shelter, go to the basement of a building."*

Notes in a research journal:

- Underground shelter
- Basement
- Stay away from windows
- Small room
- Bathtub

Modeled Writing

At the first sign of a tornado, it's important for you to stop whatever you are doing and find a safe shelter. If your house has an <u>underground</u> shelter, go there quickly. An underground shelter is the safest place to be during a tornado.

If you don't have access to an underground tornado shelter, go to the <u>basement</u> of a building. Be sure to <u>stay away from windows</u>, as glass may break during a tornado.

- Choosing words that evoke strong images

    - *Informative and explanatory writing doesn't have to sound like an encyclopedia. Using vivid verbs and strong adjectives will make my piece more interesting and fun to read. Watch as I choose my words carefully in this piece.*

Modeled Writing

"Glacier caves" are formed when the <u>thick, dense</u> ice inside the glacier begins to melt. As the water <u>melts,</u> it <u>drips</u> and <u>carves</u> caves and tunnels inside the ice.

- Anticipating the questions of your reader

    - *After reading this section in my piece about rattlesnakes, I think my reader will be wondering, "What should a person do if he is bitten by a rattlesnake?" I think I'll add that information next. Thinking about the questions my reader might have helps me as I write.*

- Using headings to group information

    - *Most informative or explanatory texts use headings to group information together and help a reader navigate the text easily. Watch me as I insert headings in this piece on geysers.*

- Using visuals

    - *I've written about the importance of wearing a seatbelt, and now I'm thinking that I want to add a visual to help my reader know the proper way to buckle up. Visuals are often used in informative and explanatory writing. They make the writing even clearer!*

- Adding captions to visuals

  - *I found some great photographs that show what happens when a volcano erupts. I've added them to my piece, but now I need to add a caption underneath or to the side of each photograph. The caption will tell readers what they are looking at, and it gives me another chance to teach my reader about volcanoes.*

- Including domain-specific vocabulary and bold words

  - *I'm working on a piece about monarch butterflies, and I want to include some words that are specific to the life cycle of a butterfly, such as "chrysalis," "caterpillar," and "metamorphosis." Those are important words to know if you are learning about butterflies. When I include them, I'll make them boldface so my reader will know that these words are important to this topic.*

Modeled Writing

Once the **caterpillar** has eaten and grown to many times its size, it turns into a **chrysalis.** The caterpillar is going through several amazing changes at this stage. These change are called **metamorphosis**.

Personal narrative writing

- Establishing the setting

  - *When we write personal narratives, we need to make sure our reader knows where we were and what was going on around us when this experience happened—we need to talk about the setting. I'm writing about the time I watched an amazing meteor shower. It was at night and I was far away from the lights of the town so there was blackness all around me. Watch as I get some of those things down on my page.*

Modeled Writing

The sun had long since set and, far away from the lights of the city, the blackness of night surrounded us. I stifled a yawn and searched the sky.

- Using temporal words to signal event order

- ▪ *When I write about an event, I need to include words that tell my reader when things happened. Words like "next," "finally," and "before that" can be used to help my writing make sense. Watch me as I use some of those words in this piece about my bike wreck.*

- • Choosing words that evoke strong images

  - ▪ *For this piece, I want my readers to feel like they are right there in the field with me, looking up at the meteor shower. Listen as I think about the field—what I saw and heard and felt that night. I want to add these words so that my readers will be able to visualize what happened. I remember that it was cold, and I was glad I had brought a blanket. I also remember that the grass was really scratchy on my back and legs. I think I'll write a bit about the cold and the scratchy grass. When I describe what I felt, saw, and heard, it helps my readers feel like they are there with me.*

Modeled Writing

The grass was scratchy on my back and legs, and I wished I had heeded my friend's advice and brought a blanket. A slight breeze cooled the night air but also carried with it the smell of a recent rain shower. The clouds had cleared and the sky was alive with a million particles of light.

- • Creating a satisfying ending

  - ▪ *I need to think about how to end this piece of writing. I could just say, "That's what happened when I saw the meteor shower," but I think I can do better than that. I want my ending to be like the bow on top of a present that I have given my reader. Sometimes a good ending reveals the feelings or reactions of the writer. As I think back to that night, I remember thinking that I had never seen something so amazing. It really had an impact on me. So I think I'll say: "I've seen many amazing things in nature, but I've never seen something that made such an impact on me. I'll never forget the night on the mountain under the stars."*

- • Varying sentence lengths

  - ▪ *When I'm writing, I want to think about my sentences and how they sound when I read them out loud. I don't want all of my sentences to be short, and I don't want all of them to be long. I want to mix it up—using some long and some short sentences. Watch me as I write and think about adding variety to the length of my sentences.*

- Varying sentence beginnings

  - *As I look at this fantastic paragraph from* The Relatives Came, *I notice that Cynthia Rylant used a different word to start each sentence. I think that's partly why this paragraph is so fun to read! Watch me as I craft my own paragraph and think about using a variety of sentence beginnings.*

Opinion Writing

- Choosing a powerful opinion statement

  - *I'm ready to give my opinion about whether or not kids should help out with chores at home. Choosing a powerful way to give my opinion is important when I'm writing. I could just write: "Kids should do chores." Or I could give examples and say: "Sweeping, mopping, and dusting. These are just a few of the things that need to be done to keep homes clean. It's my opinion that kids should help with these and other chores around the house."*

- Supporting your opinion with reasons and examples

  - *I've stated my opinion, but I need to give some reasons why I think kids should help with chores around the house. Watch as I use a sticky note to make a list of all the reasons why I think kids should help with chores.*

Why kids should help with chores:

- Fosters responsibility

- Part of being in a family

- Learn life skills

- Gain a feeling of accomplishment

- More time for family fun if everyone chips in

- Choosing and using only your strongest reasons

  - *Now that I've made a list of reasons why I think kids should help with chores, I'm going to rate each of my reasons. When I begin writing, I want to use only my strongest reasons. If a reason is really strong, I'll give it a 4. I'll give it a 2 or a 3 if it's a fairly strong reason and a 1 if it's a weak reason. Once I've rated my reasons, I'll write about only those reasons that are the strongest.*

- Using linking words to link opinion and reasons

  - *Words like "additionally," "for example," and "consequently" join one idea to the next. When we are giving an opinion, we can use these words to connect our opinion with the reasons that support our opinion. As I write about why I think kids should help with chores, I'm going to include some linking words.*

Modeled Writing

When kids help out with household chores, they learn life skills that will help them when they are on their own as adults. For example, doing laundry is something that all people need to learn at some point in their lives. Why not learn how to do it now?

- Providing logically ordered reasons that are supported by facts, details, or examples

  - *I want to organize my reasons in a way that makes sense to my reader. I'm going to begin with one of my strongest reasons— that doing chores gives kids a sense of accomplishment. Watch me as I write: "Everyone needs to feel a sense of accomplishment. It's good for the soul…." Now I'll add some details or examples about this to make the paragraph organized and clear. I can say something about how starting and finishing a job led to that satisfaction. Watch me as I do that.*

Modeled Writing

Everyone needs to feel a sense of accomplishment. It's good for the soul! When kids help out with household chores, they get the satisfaction of starting and finishing a job and they can see the results of their labor. For example, it can be rewarding to see a huge pile of dirty laundry slowly disappear as each load is folded and put away neatly in drawers.

- Crafting a powerful conclusion

  - *I'm ready to wrap up my opinion, and I want to write something that will stick in the reader's mind. Maybe I'll write: "Chores: They teach responsibility and help kids feel good about themselves and their contributions to the family. So let's get cleaning!"*

> Revision asks us to step away from our writing and look at it again through the eyes of the reader.

The Courage to Revise

It's true that revision is something that all writers need to do, but it's also true that revision is something that most student writers *loathe* to do.

Many of our students see revision as a necessary evil, a box to check off on the list of steps in the writing process—you know, the step that occurs right after *drafting* and before *editing*. Often, students don't value the power of revision because they don't understand what it is or why we do it. As teachers of writing, we need to come alongside our students and model how real writers approach revision.

First, let's make sure we are clear about the difference between *editing* and *revising*. Editing deals mainly with mechanics. When you edit, you look for anything to which a professional proofreader would attend: spelling, capitalization, punctuation, etc. In other words, you're working with conventions of writing when you edit.

Revision, on the other hand, deals primarily with content and craft, structure and sentence fluency—the "guts" of the writing. It doesn't matter if the conventions are picture perfect if the content isn't clear and inviting. "Revision," in its most literal sense, means to "see again," to "re-vision." Revision asks us to step away from our writing and look at it again through the eyes of the reader.

Next, we need to rethink the notion that revision is simply one step in the writing process. I used to think the writing process went something like this:

1. Brainstorm
2. Prewrite
3. Draft
4. Revise
5. Edit
6. Publish

However, the longer I work with student writers and the more I write myself, my view of revision (and the entire writing process) is changing. My current thinking is that the writing process actually looks more like this:

1. Revise
2. Revise
3. Revise
4. Revise
5. Revise
6. Revise

When we revise, we ask questions, such as "Will this make sense? Did I make my point clear for the reader? Will my reader want to keep reading?" We ask these questions after we have completed the piece, for certain, but we also ask these questions while we are drafting—and sometimes even *before* we put pen to paper (or fingers to keyboard).

As we think aloud and model our own writing for our students, we need to be courageous enough to revise our own work. I use the word "courageous" because revision takes courage. It takes courage to take an honest look at a draft and see what needs to be changed. It takes courage to let go of a word, a sentence, a paragraph that took so much of our time and energy to write. In short, it takes courage to admit that we (and our drafts) are not perfect.

Donald Graves (1994) once said, "Children don't suddenly make good judgments about what strikes them in a piece of writing. The quality of what they observe is the result of sound mini-lessons."

Here are some examples of things I say during mini-lessons to show students what I'm thinking as I revise:

> First draft: My grandmother and I used to love to sit on her front porch swing and rock. Sometimes, we would eat Popsicles and sometimes we would just hold hands and talk.

I've written about one of my favorite memories of my grandmother: she and I sitting on her front porch swing. I've written a couple of sentences, but there aren't many sensory details that really bring this moment to life for my reader. I don't think my reader will be able to picture what I was seeing, feeling, and hearing in that moment. I'm going to add some more details to this paragraph—I'm going to revise. Notice what I do as a writer and what changes I make to help paint a picture in my reader's mind.

> Second draft: My grandmother and I used to love to sit on her front porch swing and rock. Sometimes, we'd eat Popsicles while we rocked. The bright, red treat would melt quickly in the hot Arizona sun, and we'd giggle as we tried to keep the stickiness from dripping onto our legs. Other times, we would simply hold hands and rock together while she sang. I can still feel her rough, weathered hands in mine and hear her sweet voice keeping time with the creaks of the swing.

First draft: Our town needs a new community pool. The pool near Bogert Park is old and run down. As a result, it's often closed for repairs, leaving no public pool for people to enjoy. Furthermore, the current pool requires much more water than the newer, more modern pools. So it's wasting our town's precious water! We need a new pool.

Sincerely,
Kelly Boswell

I've finished my persuasive letter to the city commissioners about the need for a new community pool, but my ending sounds dull. There's nothing there to make the readers think or take action. This needs some work! Watch me as I look at our mentor texts to see how those writers ended their persuasive texts and then use those ideas to revise my work.

Second draft: Our town needs a new community pool. The pool near Bogert Park is old and run down. As a result, it's often closed for repairs, leaving no public pool for people to enjoy. Furthermore, the current pool requires much more water than the newer, more modern pools. So it's wasting our town's precious water! As you can see, there are many good reasons to construct a new community pool. Our whole town will benefit! I hope that you'll consider it.

Sincerely,
Kelly Boswell

First draft: Penguins are black and white. It helps them be camouflaged. Their backs are black. That helps them blend into the water. Predators can't see them. Penguin front sides are white. The white looks like the surface of the water. The fish below them can't see them.

I just read this paragraph out loud to hear how it sounds, and it's pretty choppy. It should flow when my reader reads it, and it's not flowing now. I need to revise! Watch me as I revise some of the sentence lengths in order to make it more engaging.

Second draft: Penguins are black and white, which helps them be camouflaged. Their backs are black, and that helps them blend into the water so predators can't see them. Penguin front sides are white. The white side looks like the surface of the water, which helps them hunt because the fish below them can't see them.

Students will be much more motivated to do the hard work of revision if they see another writer (namely *you*) do it. If we, as adult writers, are willing to be vulnerable, share our drafts, and rework some things that need attention, our students will be willing to do the same. By investing in our writing and our readers through modeling, we create a nonthreatening environment where it is safe to play around with words and try things out—to be a writer in process.

Revision strategies that I use myself:

- Read the writing out loud to hear how it sounds.

- Reread constantly.

- Take a break from the writing (24–48 hours), and read it again with the eyes of a reader.

- Ask questions as I reread: *Does this sound the way I want it to? Is it interesting?*

- Take something out.

- Move paragraphs (or whole sections) around.

- Add words to make it more interesting or easier to understand.

- Reread with a focus on organization.

Give Audience and Purpose Center Stage

Ursula K. Le Guin once said, "The unread story is not a story; it is little black marks on wood pulp. The reader, reading it, makes it live: a live thing, a story."

Ask any elementary teacher about her goals for the readers in her classroom, and my guess is that, at some point, he or she will say something like, "I want them to be lifelong readers—to love reading and to see the value of reading for pleasure and as a way to be informed citizens." That's a fine goal, wouldn't you agree?

So here's a question to ponder: What are our goals for the *writers* in our classroom? Of course we want them to capitalize the beginning of a sentence and punctuate that sentence correctly. But beyond all that—beyond the mechanics and the organization and the satisfying conclusion, don't we ultimately want them to become lifelong writers? Don't we want them to love writing and to see the value of writing as a tool to reflect, to learn, and to remember? Don't we want our students to have a voice in the ever-expanding digital age, where writing is taking center stage like never before? For me, that is the ultimate goal for each writer in my classroom—to become a person who values writing and uses writing in his or her daily life.

So, what kinds of writing do we do as lifelong writers? In Chapter 3, I asked you to think of the last five pieces of writing you had crafted. Here's my list:

Kind of writing	Audience	Purpose
to-do list	myself	to help me remember what I needed to accomplish today
text	my husband	to ask him to pick up something that we needed from the store
e-mail	the curriculum director at a school where I will be visiting	to verify the agenda and to let her know what supplies we'll need for the staff development session
procedural directions	my son's classroom teacher and school nurse	to inform them about my son's food allergy and provide an action plan in case he ingests something with peanuts
thank-you card	my parents	to thank them for the gift they sent to my husband and me for our anniversary

Out of curiosity, I asked my husband, who works as a portfolio manager, to do the same. Here are his last five pieces of writing:

Kind of writing	Audience	Purpose
notes from a meeting	myself	to help me remember what was discussed
memo	executive committee	to persuade them to buy a piece of equipment
report (including tables, graphs, and text)	limited partners	to report on operational costs for the month of July
e-mail	office administrator	to ask if she could reschedule a meeting
text	my sister	to ask her to call me

When I examined both of our lists, something stood out to me: In the real world, we write to *people*, not to *prompts*. As lifelong writers, we typically write to a very specific audience for a very specific purpose. As writers, we research, write, revise, and edit, and we do it all with the purpose and audience in the forefront of our minds. I would venture to say that, for many of us, if we don't value the audience and aren't invested in the purpose, we typically don't write at all.

However, I find that much of the writing that students do in school is devoid of a real audience or genuine purpose. As I reflect on my own teaching, there were times when the audience was the teacher (me) and the purpose was a grade in my grade book. While that may have been motivating for some students, it didn't motivate the vast majority of them.

These days, when teachers tell me that one of their greatest challenges is motivating their students to write, my first question is often: *What kinds of writing are you asking them to do? Where does the writing go? Is there an audience for the writing, or is it simply turned in for a grade?*

Motivation isn't the only thing that suffers when students are given writing tasks that lack an authentic audience and purpose. The quality of their writing is also diminished. Regie Routman, in her book *Writing Essentials* (2005), says, "Often the writing that students do freely at home, which emerges from their own interests, far exceeds the quality of work and effort they put into school writing, which they mostly see as mechanical and routine."

In fact, research clearly shows that students are more likely to become proficient readers who *enjoy* writing if they have some choice of topic and audience and they value the writing purpose (Graves 1994; Ball and Farr 2003; Routman, 2000).

It's clear, isn't it? If we are going to prepare students for the real world of writing, we need to model how we consider audience and purpose in our own writing.

Here are some examples of things I say to students to show them how I think about my audience and purpose for writing each time I write:

> *I've decided to write my personal narrative about the time when my dad helped me change my first flat tire. We had a lot of mishaps, and when the tire was changed, we both collapsed in a tired heap on the grass next to my car.*
>
> *I could just write this piece for me, but I think my dad would love this. When the piece is finished, I think I'll give it to him, along with a note of thanks for being a great dad. I think he would treasure it too.*

> *I'm writing this explanatory poster about how to stay safe in a tornado. As I've been writing, I've been thinking about where this piece could go when it's finished. I think I could display it in our town's community center. People use that building often, and it might be a great place to display it.*

> *I'm going to write an opinion piece about the importance of kids helping out with household chores. I'm going to write with my own children in mind because they need some convincing! When I'm finished with this piece, I'm going to give it to my boys. Maybe after reading it, they'll be more enthusiastic about doing their chores.*

When we think aloud and model how we consider our audience and purpose, we send a clear message: Writers write for readers.

As writing teachers, we also need to set a clear purpose and establish a real audience for the writing that our students produce throughout the school year. Penny Kittle (2013), author, teacher, and literacy coach, says that her goal is create a classroom where "every writer will experience the electricity of investing in writing that says something vital to the reader." Our goal should be the same.

Below are some examples of traditional classroom writing tasks along with ideas for tweaking them so that students have a clear purpose and are writing for a real audience. I've also included some options from which students can choose. It's not important that the students in my class are *all* writing the *same* thing. What's important is that students are thinking, talking, and writing with a clear purpose in mind and for an audience that matters to them.

Instead of a...	Why not a...	Possible audience	Other choices for student writing
book report	book review	• With parent permission, students can share their reviews online for a larger audience. • Reviews can be placed on the inside cover of books in the classroom library. • Video record students sharing their book reviews. Then show the "commercials" as part of a slide show that is played during open house or during the school's book fair.	• letter to the author of the book • blog entry about the book • author chat or interview
state report	travel brochure	• Brochures can be duplicated and then displayed at a local travel agency. • Students can set up a "summer travel ideas" area in the foyer of the school as the school year ends. Families can browse the travel brochures for interesting places to visit.	• electronic slide show • children's book for younger students

Instead of a...	Why not a...	Possible audience	Other choices for student writing
set of procedural directions (i.e., how to brush your teeth or how to make a sandwich)	set of procedural directions for substitute teachers or new students (e.g., how we handle bullying at our school or the steps of our dismissal routine each day)	• Procedures can be part of the plans that teachers leave for substitutes. (Teachers would still craft the lesson plans, but students could write the procedures for things that never change, such as how dismissal works or how the class takes attendance.) • School procedures can be published into a school guidebook and given to substitute teachers and new families when they come to the building. • Guidebooks can also be given to Realtors who are showing homes in that school's attendance area.	• posters explaining how to do something that the student is an expert in (e.g., skateboarding, origami, knitting) • posters (and activities) can be shared among classmates during an "expert celebration" • a "how-to" on how to use some handy apps on an electronic device that can be shared with parents or caregivers
friendly letter	persuasive letter	• Letters can be written to the chamber of commerce, city commissioners, or the local newspaper to suggest changes for the school or community. • Students can craft letters to local businesses, asking for donations for school events (i.e., book donations for school literacy nights or food and beverage donations for a school carnival).	• Instead of letters of complaints, why not invite students to write a letter of thanks to a company that makes a favorite product?

In this chapter, I provided you with a list of some of the skills that I model when working with students. The ideas presented here are by no means exhaustive, but I hope you'll use them as a springboard for the modeled writing lessons in your own classroom. Above all, make sure your students are invested in the writing they are doing. Focus first on writing for real readers and creating meaningful pieces of writing. Then you can teach the skills necessary to support that writing. The two go hand in hand.

Chapter 6:
MODEL HIGH-QUALITY WRITING

"As teachers of writing, we can't just write. We have
to write so that we come to understand what it is that
we are teaching. We have to push ourselves to
notice and to understand what's happening when
we write, so that our writing becomes a powerful
curriculum tool for our teaching."

— Katie Wood Ray

Do you remember learning to drive? Chances are the process went
something like this:

You were an observant passenger.

- Sure, you weren't behind the wheel yet, but you were carefully
  observing those around you who were driving. You watched to see
  how the "experts" did it.

You took a class.

- Remember those driver's education videos? I vividly recall one in
  which the camera followed a bouncy red ball as it rolled across the
  street. The narrator's voice sharply warned, "Stop! A ball is in the
  road. Be aware! A small child may be following."

You received your learner's permit.

- Finally behind the wheel, you practiced driving while a parent sat
  next to you. Your mom (or in my case, dad) took deep breaths,
  slammed on an invisible brake on her side of the car, and
  whispered prayers. (Or, maybe that was just part of *my* process.) In
  any case, with loads of encouragement, practice, and time, you
  became more and more confident with your new skill.

You earned your license.

- Whether the world was ready or not, you received your driver's license and hit the road…or hit some mailboxes! You were still learning, but you were on your own! And when you did experience the occasional run-ins with the mailbox, you reflected: *What did I learn? How can I use this information to help me in the future?*

This process sounds a lot like the Gradual Release of Responsibility, doesn't it? In the Gradual Release of Responsibility model, the learner first observes an expert, then tries the skill with someone right there to coach him. Finally, he tries the skill on his own, all the while reflecting and asking, "What did I learn? How can this help me as I move forward?"

When I was first learning to drive, I looked to the expert drivers in my family to show me how it was done. As I rode in the car with my dad, I watched him come to a complete stop and signal. I watched him slow down and pump his brakes as he navigated the Montana ice and snow.

As my dad was driving, I'm sure he wasn't thinking, "You know, Kelly is going to fail when she first starts to drive on her own. She'll let out the clutch too fast and stall the engine. She'll probably jerk and sputter when she puts it into first gear on a hill. I want her to feel good about herself as a driver, so as I drive, I think I'll just randomly stall the engine or jerk and sputter on a hill."

No! He drove like he normally drove. My dad was smart enough to know that I wasn't going to drive as well as he did right away, but he needed to give me a picture of how an expert driver…drives!

However, when I first began modeling my own thinking and writing for my first-grade students, I didn't write like an expert. In fact, I often wrote just like they wrote, mimicking the kind the writing I thought they would attempt.

For example, I would write something like this:

I like my bike. It is red. I got it for my birthday.

Sure, I was modeling my own thinking and writing, but I wasn't writing the way I normally write as an adult. I wasn't showing them how an *expert* writes. Unintentionally, I was encouraging my students to write simple (and frankly, *boring*) sentences. I hadn't meant to do that. My intentions, in fact, were completely pure. Wanting them to feel confident and successful with their own attempts at writing, I was modeling sentences that I felt most of them could successfully write on their own.

As the years passed, I realized that I needed to rethink the kind of writing I was modeling.

Each day, I would engage in one of my favorite activities: I would read aloud to my students. One day, I noticed something: When I read aloud, I didn't read like a first grader—I read like a proficient adult reader. I read with the fluency and expression of an experienced reader because my students needed to hear what an expert reader sounded like. Suddenly, it became clear: I needed to do the same thing when it came to writing. I needed to show them how an experienced writer thinks and writes, modeling writing that was a bit beyond their reach so that they could strive to achieve it.

So I began writing pieces that sounded more like as this:

> One of my most prized possessions is the sporty, blue bike that my husband gave me for my birthday. During the spring and summer months, my bike and I have many adventures!

Each time I modeled, I thought out loud while I crafted rich and interesting sentences. By doing so, I gave my students an authentic peek inside the mind of a "grown-up" writer. They saw and heard how I actually write. I wasn't expecting all of my students to be able to write this way. The truth is that many of my students were emergent readers who weren't yet able to read the sentences I had crafted (which is why I always read my sentences as I was writing and when I finished writing). After several weeks of modeling this kind of writing, I noticed something: Many of my students were trying to imitate my style, my words, and my writing. They were stretching and straining to write more interesting sentences.

The truth is, we can't expect that our students will create high-quality writing unless we have shown them what high-quality writing looks like and sounds like. They need to see a *proficient* writer in action.

Below are some examples of how you might tweak a simple sentence to make it more rich and interesting.

Instead of modeling...	Try modeling...
It was snowing.	The silent snow fell from the sky and landed lightly on my wool hat and coat. I stuck out my tongue and tasted the icy, cold crystals.
Forest fires can start when lightning strikes a tree.	A hot lightning bolt strikes a tree in the middle of the forest. The force and heat of the bolt heat the sap inside the tree to a boil. In a flashing instant, a forest fire has begun.
Bald eagles love to eat fish.	High in a tree, the sharp-clawed eagle searches the lake for fish. It plunges into the icy water and comes up with a fine, fat fish. Dinner is served.

Mentors and Modeling: A Powerful Combination

When I coauthored my first book, *Solutions for Reading Comprehension*, I was asked to compose an acknowledgments page and submit it to the publishing house. To be honest, this caused me some anxiety. I had never written an acknowledgments page and I wasn't sure where to begin. So I went into my office, pulled every professional book off of my shelves, and carefully read each page of acknowledgments, noting the features that set this kind of writing apart from others. Only after reading and examining dozens of examples did I feel ready to begin crafting my own.

Writers need to be readers in order to develop their craft. We lean on other writers for examples and support. For example, I'm guessing that many of us, before writing our first résumé, examined the résumés of others. Before my husband and I sent out our wedding invitations, you can be sure that we perused a few samples to get some ideas to use in our own. Good writers are careful and observant readers, noting and noticing what other authors do and then using what they've seen to create their own quality writing.

Kelly Gallagher (2011) uses three short sentences to remind us of how mentors and modeling work together: "She goes. I go. You go."

First, we look at another writer's work and notice what she has done. (*She goes.*) Then, we, as teachers, emulate it ourselves as we model our own thinking and writing. (*I go.*) Finally, we release the students to try it with their own writing. (*You go.*)

On the following pages, you'll find a list of some of my favorite mentor texts to use with students along with some of the skills I teach when using them. But before you share another writer's work and use it to highlight writing skills that can be emulated, here are a few important considerations:

- First and foremost, read the book aloud to your students for the simple *pleasure* of it. Resist the urge to stop during the first reading so that you can point out the quality features of the writing. Instead, allow your students to experience, savor, and enjoy the book first as a whole story. *Then*, when students have had a chance to experience it as a whole, invite them to re-examine the text with an eye for craft.

- Don't forget to use mentor texts to teach *conventions*. Teachers often use mentor texts to teach the craft of writing, but don't forget to look for interesting uses of punctuation too. It's imperative that students understand what conventions are and why authors use them; so when you invite students to notice the use of conventions, be sure to ask "why" questions. For example, ask questions, such as: *Why did Kevin Henkes use quotation marks here? Why did David Shannon use an exclamation point here? Why do you think Patricia Polacco used commas in this sentence? Why did Deborah Wiles start a new paragraph here?*

- Don't be afraid to use a familiar favorite over and over again. If a book is richly crafted, it can be used to teach many colors and shades of good writing. Invite students to revisit a class favorite again and again, noticing the striking features that make it a cherished book.

- Demonstrate how you *emulate*, rather than *imitate*, what another writer does. For example, if you're examining the strong lead found in *Whiteout! A Book About Blizzards* by Rick Thomas, you might say: *I love the way Rick Thomas starts this informative book about blizzards. He writes: "Blue-gray clouds creep into the sky. Windows glow in the growing darkness." I like the sound of "blue-gray clouds creep into the sky." I can almost picture the clouds moving slowly—creeping." I want to try something like that in my piece about eagles. I could say, "White feathers fly across the sky. Keen eyes search the field below." Did you see how I used the same kind of sentence that Rick Thomas used, but I changed it so that it worked for my topic? Writers do that—they borrow ideas from other writers and then make the ideas their own by changing them to fit their topic.*

On page 135 of the Appendix, you'll find a template to use when planning for the use of mentor texts in your classroom.

Narrative Mentor Texts

Title, author, and publisher	Use when teaching:
All Different Now: Juneteenth, the First Day of Freedom by Angela Johnson, published by Simon & Schuster Books for Young Readers	leads, strong verbs, words that evoke imagery, page layout, sentence fluency, how to stretch out a brief moment in time
All the Places to Love by Patricia MacLachlan, published by HarperCollins	descriptive language, voice, organization, varying sentence lengths
Amazing Grace by Mary Hoffman and Caroline Binch, published by Dial Books for Young Readers	narrative structure, strong conclusions
Aunt Flossie's Hats (and Crab Cakes Later) by Elizabeth Fitzgerald Howard and James E. Ransome, published by Clarion Books	dialogue, varying sentence structure, strong conclusions
Diary of Sallie Hester: A Covered Wagon Girl by Sallie Hester, published by Capstone	organization, strong verbs, varying sentence structure and lengths, captions, page layout
Each Little Bird That Sings by Deborah Wiles, published by Gulliver Books/Harcourt	strong leads, strong conclusion, varying sentence beginnings
Fly Away Home by Eve Bunting, published by Clarion Books	strong and reflective ending
Goodnight Baseball by Michael Dahl, published by Capstone	narrative structure, adding details, pictures to support text, repeated phrases, how to stretch out a brief moment in time
Goodnight Football by Michael Dahl, published by Capstone	narrative structure, adding details, pictures to support text, repeated phrases, how to stretch out a brief moment in time
Lilly's Purple Plastic Purse by Kevin Henkes, published by Greenwillow Books	dialogue, voice, strong leads, satisfying conclusions, temporal words to signal event order
Lost Little Penguin by Tracey Corderoy, published by Capstone	dialogue, voice, varying sentence beginnings, satisfying conclusions
My Name Is Yoon by Helen Recorvits, published by Frances Foster Books	varying sentence lengths, dialogue, organization, how to stretch out a brief moment in time

Title, author, and publisher	Use when teaching:
Saturdays and Teacakes by Lester Laminack, published by Peachtree Publishers, Ltd.	power of repeating words and phrases, details, voice
Silver Packages: An Appalachian Christmas Story by Cynthia Rylant, published by Orchard Books	establishing the setting, temporal words, descriptive language, varying sentence lengths, dialogue
The Rain Came Down by David Shannon, published by Blue Sky Press	repetitive pattern, cause and effect, problem/solution, use of dialogue
The Relatives Came by Cynthia Rylant, published by Bradbury Press	narrative structure, action verbs, pictures to support text
Those Shoes by Maribeth Boelts, published by Candlewick Press	leads, dialogue, descriptive language, focus, temporal words
Thunder Cake by Patricia Polacco, published by Philomel Books	vivid verbs, personal narrative structure, onomatopoeia
365 Penguins by Jean-Luc Fromental, published by Abrams Books for Young Readers	humor, dialogue, temporal words, font size and page layout experimentation, vivid verbs, repeated phrases

Informative/Explanatory Mentor Texts

Title, author, and publisher	Use when teaching:
A Rock Is Lively by Dianna Hutts Aston and Sylvia Long, published by Chronicle Books	repetitive pattern, page layout experimentation, bold words, temporal words that signal event order
All the Water in the World by George Ella Lyon and Katherine Tillotson, published by Atheneum Books for Young Readers	page layout experimentation, questions that generate interest, strong leads, strong conclusions, strong verbs
Amazing Military Robots by Sean Stewart Price, published by Capstone	strong leads, headings, captions, visuals that aid in comprehension, satisfying endings
Amazon Adventure by Layne deMarin, published by Capstone	headings, bold words, visuals that aid in comprehension

Title, author, and publisher	Use when teaching:
And Then There Were Eight: Poems about Space by Laura Purdie Salas, published by Capstone	nonfiction poetry, words that evoke strong sensory images, dialogue in poetry, page layout
Animal Spikes and Spines by Rebecca Rissman, published by Heinemann-Raintree	diagrams, repeated phrases, bold words, headings
Be the Best at Writing by Rebecca Rissman, published by Heinemann-Raintree	table of contents, headings, bold words, page layout
Body Bugs: Invisible Creatures Lurking Inside You by Jennifer Swanson, published by Capstone	strong leads, organization, domain-specific vocabulary, questions to keep writing interesting, how to speak directly to your reader, strong word choice, visuals that aid comprehension
Butterflies by Seymour Simon, published by HarperCollins	descriptive language, sentence beginnings, varied sentence lengths, photographs
Caves by Sally M. Walker, published by Lerner Publications	headings, strong leads, captions, diagrams, cross-sections, a strong conclusion
Everyone Can Learn to Ride a Bike by Chris Raschka, published by Schwartz & Wade Books	questions, how to speak directly to your reader, word choice
Going to School: Comparing Past and Present by Rebecca Rissman, published by Heinemann-Raintree	repeated phrases, headings, compare and contrast text structure
How to Teach a Slug to Read by Susan Pearson, published by Marshall Cavendish Children	structure of procedural texts, numbered steps, how to start each step with a verb, speech bubbles
Not All Birds Fly by Jaclyn Crupi, published by Capstone	headings, sentence beginnings, varied sentence lengths, diagrams, page layout
One Tiny Turtle by Nicola Davies, published by Candlewick Press	nonfiction narrative structure, sensory details, strong word choice, strong leads
Polar Bear, Arctic Hare: Poems of the Frozen North by Eileen Spinelli, published by Wordsong	informational poetry, descriptive language, strong verbs, words that evoke strong images
Rain Forest Animal Adaptations by Lisa J. Amstutz, published by Capstone	sentence beginnings, transition words, headings

Title, author, and publisher	Use when teaching:
See What a Seal Can Do by Chris Butterworth, published by Candlewick Press	strong leads, how to speak directly to your reader, descriptive language, strong verbs, a variety of sentence beginnings
Southeast Indians by Andrew Santella, published by Heinemann-Raintree	maps that aid in comprehension, headings, dialogue, bold words, captions, temporal words
Spiders by Nic Bishop, published by Scholastic Nonfiction	page layout, captions, interesting details, strong word choice
Step-by-Step Science Experiments in Astronomy by Janice VanCleave, published by Rosen Publishing	procedural text structure, visuals that aid in comprehension, headings
The Construction Alphabet Book by Jerry Pallotta, published by Charlesbridge	onomatopoeia, commas in a series, a variety of conventions, interesting details
The Day the Earth Stood Still by Isabel Thomas, published by Raintree	bold words, flowcharts, glossaries
The Human Head by Kathy Allen, published by Capstone	questions that generate interest, how to speak directly to your reader, insets, interesting facts
Throw Your Tooth on the Roof: Tooth Traditions from Around the World by Selby B. Beeler, published by Houghton Mifflin Co.	first-person narrative, headings, quotation marks, strong conclusions, diagrams
Walk On! A Guide for Babies of All Ages by Marla Frazee, published by Harcourt	structure of procedural texts, how to speak directly to your reader, questions, page layout experimentation
Whiteout!: A Book About Blizzards by Rick Thomas, published by Capstone	establishing the setting, vivid verbs, descriptive language, headings, how to speak directly to your reader
Why I Sneeze, Shiver, Hiccup, and Yawn by Melvin Berger, published by HarperCollins	paragraphing, topic sentence and supporting details, diagrams, using a variety of sentence beginnings, varying sentence lengths, how to speak directly to your reader

Opinion Mentor Texts

Title, author, and publisher	Use when teaching:
A Pig Parade Is a Terrible Idea by Michael Ian Black, published by Simon & Schuster Books for Young Readers	questions, how to speak directly to your reader, linking words for opinion writing, strong word choice, repetitive phrases
Can I Keep Him? by Steven Kellogg, published by Dial Press	repetitive pattern, reasons for an opinion, humor
Dear Katie, the Volcano Is a Girl by Jean Craighead George, published by Hyperion Books for Children	evidence, reasons for an opinion, considering other perspectives
Don't Let the Pigeon Drive the Bus! by Mo Willems, published by Hyperion Books for Children	other perspectives, questions, voice
Earrings! by Judith Viorst, published by Atheneum Books for Young Readers	repetitive pattern, reasons for an opinion, voice
Hey, Little Ant by Phillip and Hannah Hoose, published by Tricycle Press	reasons for an opinion, voice, other perspectives
How Can We Help Out in Our Community? by Tony Stead, published by Capstone	text structure, reasons for an opinion, illustrations
How Much Time Should Kids Spend Online? by Tony Stead, published by Capstone	text structure, reasons for an opinion, illustrations
I Wanna Iguana by Karen Kaufman Orloff, published by Putnam	format of a persuasive letter, reasons for an opinion
My Teacher for President by Kay Winters, published by Dutton Children's Books	reasons for an opinion, format of a persuasive letter
Pick a Picture, Write an Opinion! by Kristen McCurry, published by Capstone	structure of an opinion, headings, page layout, photographs
Should Children Have Homework? by Tony Stead, published by Capstone	text structure, reasons for an opinion, illustrations

Title, author, and publisher	Use when teaching:
Should There Be Zoos?: A Persuasive Text by Tony Stead, published by Mondo Publishing	text structure, considering other perspectives, reasons for an opinion
Should We Squash Bugs? by Tony Stead, published by Capstone	text structure, reasons for an opinion, illustrations
The Perfect Pet by Margie Palatini and Bruce Whatley, published by HarperCollins	repetitive pattern, reasons for an opinion, humor
The Perfect Puppy for Me! by Jane O'Connor, published by Viking	evidence, reasons for an opinion, questions
The Pigeon Wants a Puppy! by Mo Willems, published by Hyperion Books for Children	questions, how to speak directly to your reader, voice
What Is the Best Pet? by Tony Stead, published by Capstone	text structure, reasons for an opinion, illustrations
What's Your Favorite Animal? by Eric Carle and Friends, published by Henry Holt and Company	narrative structure within an opinion, text structure, page layout experimentation
Why Should We Recycle? by Tony Stead, published by Capstone	text structure, reasons for an opinion, illustrations

Years ago, I attended a conference and had the opportunity to hear from Lois Burdett, a second-grade teacher at Hamlet Public School in Stratford, Ontario.

Inspired by the name of her school and town, she began to introduce the works of Shakespeare to her young students. The seven- and eight-year-olds in her classroom read many of his plays and even performed several of them for the townspeople. In short, she began to immerse them in Shakespeare's writing.

Throughout her presentation, she shared several samples of student writing from her classroom. As I examined the writing samples, it became abundantly clear that many of her students were beginning to emulate Shakespeare's style. No, they weren't crafting long works of tragedy and comedy, but their writing revealed a playfulness with language. The sentences were rich and complex. The verbs were vivid and the vocabulary that they included in their writing reached far beyond second grade.

At the conclusion of her session, she urged us to immerse our students in quality literature, to expose them to rich and descriptive language, and to model our own thinking and writing as we emulate and learn from other writers.

She reminded us that if students receive a steady diet of simple text, they will create simple text when they write. On the other hand, if students receive a steady and varied diet of richly-crafted and powerful books, they are much more likely to create high-quality writing themselves.

Chapter 7:

SAMPLE LESSONS

Throughout this book, I've provided the think-alouds and teacher language that can be used when modeling your own thinking and writing. But I have yet to show you how modeled writing fits into one *whole* writing lesson. In this chapter, I have compiled several mini-lessons that highlight the use of modeled writing. Each lesson is designed to be taught in eight to 10 minutes and can be slipped right into the daily writing block.

The lessons have been divided into three grade-level groupings—grades K–1, grades 2–3, and grades 4–5. Within each grade-level grouping, you'll find a lesson connected to three text types: opinion, informative/explanatory, and personal narrative. These lessons are not designed to teach the features and structures found in a particular text type. Rather, they are designed to teach a specific skill that supports the text type.

Each mini-lesson is set up using the same elements and structure:

Lesson focus

- The beginning of each lesson identifies a single, specific, and narrow focus. This focus sets the tone for the think-aloud, partner talk, and modeled writing.

Charts and lists

- Some of the lessons include an anchor chart or list with words, phrases, or ideas that can support students when they are writing independently. These charts and lists are simply samples, and I encourage you to create the charts or lists *with the students*—inviting them to examine the published books in your classrooms to see what other writers have done.

- Once you've created the anchor chart or list, leave it up where students can see it and access it during independent writing. And be sure to model how *you* use them to help craft your sentences too.

Step-by-step suggestions

- Embedded in each mini-lesson are three steps to follow. Each step provides you with clear direction so that you can keep the mini-lesson mini. Remember, powerful mini-lessons are brief and focused.

Think-alouds

- Each lesson contains examples of teacher language that can be used as you model. Use the language exactly as provided, or make it your own by adding your own words and style. The important thing is that you make your thinking visible to students as you write.

Partner talk

- Sprinkled throughout the mini-lessons are opportunities for students to talk with a partner about what they are noticing and thinking. I provided some questions to use to prompt discussion, but you may wish to tweak these to meet the needs of your students.

- It's helpful to listen in while partners are talking, but keep in mind that these are *modeled* writing experiences rather than *shared* writing experiences. You might listen to the students' ideas, but you are in the driver's seat—deciding what to add to your piece of writing.

Reflection

- In the reflection section, the focus of the lesson is restated and the students are invited to try out the skill during independent writing time.

Modeled writing

- Each mini-lesson includes modeled writing samples. Use the samples as they are, or use them as a springboard for creating your own pieces of writing.

- It's important to remember that in a modeled writing lesson, you are creating a piece of writing *in front of students*, so don't give in to the temptation to simply display my modeled writing and explain what was done. Jump in and create your own!

My hope is that these lessons will serve as a catalyst for you to begin creating your own modeled writing mini-lessons. On pages 136–139 of the Appendix are samples of templates you can use when planning daily or weekly mini-lessons.

Grades: K–1

TEXT TYPE: Opinion
LESSON FOCUS: Supply a Reason for Your Opinion

STEP 1: Think aloud as you write an opinion, and think about a reason that supports your opinion.

Think-aloud: We've been doing some thinking and talking about which animal makes the best pet, and we each have our own opinions about it. My opinion is that fish make the best pets. Watch me as I write that. (Write: "Fish make the best pets.") I could add a period and end my sentence there, but I'm guessing that my reader might be wondering <u>why</u> I think fish make the best pets. I need to give a reason for my opinion. When I give a reason for my opinion, it makes my writing much more powerful.

I think fish make the best pets because they are so easy to care for. I'm going to write the word "because" and then I'll write "they are easy to care for." I think I'll add a couple more sentences about that. I could say, "You need to clean their tank and feed them, but they don't need a lot of time and attention." Watch me as I get that down on the page.

Partner talk: Let's read what I've written so far. What do you think? Talk with your partner about what you notice.

STEP 2: Model how you consider an additional reason, and add it to your piece.

Think-aloud: I like these sentences, and I think my reader will too. Now, to make my writing even better, I think I'll give another reason why I think fish make the best pets. I think fish make the best pets because people often feel relaxed when they watch fish. So having a fish might help a person relax! I'm going to use the word "also" to start my next sentence. I think I'll say, "Also, some people think it's relaxing to watch fish swim around." Watch me as I add that reason to my writing.

Partner talk: Let's reread my writing together. How did adding my reasons improve my writing? If this were your piece of writing, would you add anything else to make it better?

STEP 3: Reread and reflect.

Think-aloud: I'm really happy with my writing. I've given my opinion, and I've told my reader <u>why</u> I feel that way. I think these reasons will help my reader think about fish in a new way. It's important to add some reasons when you are writing opinions.

Reflection: Today I showed you how writers give an opinion about something and give reasons for their opinion. When we do that, we give our readers something to think about and it makes our opinion stronger! As you write today, think about the reasons you can give to support your opinion. Who's ready to get started?

Modeled writing

Fish make great pets because they are easy to care for. You need to clean their tanks and feed them, but they don't need a lot of time and attention. Also, some people think it's relaxing to watch fish swim around. If you're ever feeling grouchy, you can make yourself comfortable, watch your fish, and feel the grouchiness float away.

Grades: K–1

TEXT TYPE: Informative/Explanatory
LESSON FOCUS: Provide a Sense of Closure

Before the lesson, gather a few quality nonfiction picture books that contain strong endings. Possible mentor texts might include the following, published by Capstone:

Volcano Explorers by Pam Rosenberg
Rain Forest Life by Janine Scott
Space by Martha E. H. Rustad

STEP 1: Reread your piece of writing. Pause before the ending and think about how you can bring closure to the piece.

Think-aloud: I've written about what plants need to survive and grow, and now I'm ready to end my writing. Let's see. I could write, "The End," but I think I can do better than that. I could say: "That's all I know about what plants need."

Partner talk: What do you think about this ending? Is it interesting? Put your heads together: Can you think of another way to end this piece?

STEP 2: Examine mentor texts and think aloud about other possible endings.

Think-aloud: I have a few nonfiction books there. Let's look at the way these authors ended their writing. (Read the ending from each one.) This author used a question to end her writing. As a reader, it's fun to think about traveling into space myself someday. This author invites the reader to think about what new animals we might find in the future. That's another interesting way to end the writing. As I look at these endings, it helps me think about my own writing.

Partner talk: Now that we've looked at the way other authors ended their writing, can you think of another way I could end this piece?

STEP 3: Try out several different endings and decide which one works best.

Think-aloud: Some authors speak right to the reader at the end of their pieces. Maybe I'll try that. I could say, "If you have patience, you can plant a seed and watch it grow." Here is another one I could try: "Now that you know what plants need to survive, you're ready to grow your own plants." Those are okay, but I think I want to talk a little bit about what plants do for us. Plants grow inside and outside, and they make our homes and yards more beautiful. So I think I'll write: "Plants are everywhere around us. They make our planet and our homes more beautiful. So take care of your plants and watch them grow!" I like this ending and I think my reader will like it too. Watch me as I write it. (Write the ending.)

Reflection: Did you see how I did that? Did you notice how I looked to see what other writers did to end their writing? Did you notice how I tried several different endings out loud to hear how they sounded before I chose one to write?

Today, I showed you how writers choose their words carefully when they are ending a piece of writing. A good ending helps your reader think more deeply about your topic. As you work on your own writing today, think about how you might wrap it up in a way that is interesting. Off we go!

Modeled writing

First draft:
We see plants all around us, but how do they grow? Plants need special things to help them live and grow. First, plants need healthy soil and fresh water. Sunlight is also needed for plants to grow. Just like us, plants also need food! There's one more thing that plants need to grow—time! Most plants do not grow overnight, so growing plants takes patience.

Revised draft:
We see plants all around us, but how do they grow? Plants need special things to help them live and grow. First, plants need healthy soil and fresh water. Sunlight is also needed for plants to grow. Just like us, plants also need food! There's one more thing that plants need to grow—time! Most plants do not grow overnight, so growing plants takes patience. **Plants are everywhere around us. They make our planet and our homes more beautiful. So take care of your plants and watch them grow!**

Grades: K–1

TEXT TYPE: Personal Narrative

LESSON FOCUS: Add Details to Strengthen Writing

STEP 1: Tell a short story, using lots of interesting details.

Think-aloud: One day, I was on a really long hike with my husband. The temperature was 90 degrees that day and, as we walked, I was getting hotter and hotter. It felt like the sun was scorching the ground! My shirt was sticking to my back and the water in my water bottle was warm and not very refreshing. All of a sudden, I spotted a mountain stream up ahead! I hustled over to it, kicked off my shoes and socks, and walked right into the river. The water was icy cold and it felt so good!

Now watch me as I write that story here on the page. (Write: "I was really hot, so it felt good to put my feet in the river.")

Partner talk: Do you notice any details that are missing in my writing? What's missing?

STEP 2: Write the narrative again, thinking aloud as you add details to strengthen the writing.

Think-aloud: I'm going to write my narrative again, but this time I'm going to try to include all of those details that I included when I told you my story. I remember that I was really hot. I could just write: "I was hot," but when I told you the story, I talked about how it felt: The sun was scorching the ground and my shirt was sticking to my back. Watch as I get that down on the page. (Write: "The sun was scorching the ground under my feet, and my shirt was sticking to my back.") I like that! Those details help the reader picture what it was like that day. Next, I'll add the part about the warm water in my water bottle. I'll say: "I took a drink from my water bottle, but it was warm from hours in the sun." That detail really helps you understand how hot it was, doesn't it?

Partner talk: Let's read what I have so far. What do you think? Is it better than my first piece of writing? Why?

STEP 3: Continue writing, thinking aloud as you add details.

Think-aloud: Now I'll tell about seeing the river and putting my feet in. If I think back to my story, I remember that I saw a mountain stream up ahead and I hurried toward it. I think I'll say: "Suddenly, I saw a mountain stream up ahead. I hurried to the water's edge and kicked off my shoes and socks. With my bare feet, I tiptoed into the river." The details that I'm adding will help put a picture in the reader's mind. In other words, my reader will be able to visualize what happened to me that day. That's what details do!

Reflection: Reread both drafts and reflect on the value of the added details.

Let's read my first draft again and then read my next draft. Which piece of writing do you like better? I agree! The second draft is much more interesting to read, isn't it? When I added all of those interesting details, it made my writing sparkle!

Today, as you tell and write your stories, think about adding lots of details to your writing. Who thinks they can try that today?

Modeled writing

First draft:
I was really hot, so it felt good to put my feet in the river.

Second draft:
The sun was scorching the ground under my feet, and my shirt was sticking to my back. I took a drink from my water bottle, but it was warm from hours in the sun. Suddenly, I saw a mountain stream up ahead. I hurried to the water's edge and kicked off my shoes and socks. With my bare feet, I tiptoed into the river. The icy cold water felt so good!

Grades: 2–3

TEXT TYPE: Opinion

LESSON FOCUS: Introduce the Topic and State an Opinion

In advance of the lesson, create a chart of sentence starters for opinion writing (like those shown on page 99). Or invite students to identify sentence starters in opinion mentor texts and create the chart *with* students.

STEP 1: Think aloud about a topic.

> *Think-aloud: Today, I want to show you how I introduce a topic and then give my opinion on that topic. I've been thinking a lot about whether or not kids should have chores at home. Some people think that kids work hard enough at school and that they should be able to relax when they are home. Other people think it's good for kids to help out at home because it teaches them responsibility.*

> *Partner talk: Think for a moment. What is your opinion on this topic? Do you think kids should have chores at home or not? Talk with your partner, and share your opinion.*

STEP 2: Think aloud as you model how to introduce a topic.

> *Think-aloud: I can tell that each of you have an opinion on this topic, and so do I! I think kids should help out at home by doing chores. I want to write about that opinion, but first I want to introduce the topic for my reader. It wouldn't make sense for me to start by writing: "I think kids should do chores." It just comes out of nowhere! Instead, I need to introduce the topic so that my reader is ready for my opinion. Let's see…I could say: "Chores are a part of every household and every family, but who should do the chores?" Or I could start by saying: "Sweeping, mopping, and scrubbing the toilet—these are just a few of the many tasks that need to be done to keep the house clean."*

> *Partner talk: Which introduction do you prefer? Is there another way I could introduce the topic of household chores?*

STEP 3: Write the introductory sentence and your opinion.

Think-aloud: I like my second introduction better. It introduces the topic of chores, and it helps set up my opinion. Watch me as I write that.

Now I'm ready to state my opinion on this topic. Our chart is filled with different sentence starters I could use. Listen as I try a few of them out loud: "I believe kids should be sharing the load…," "I think kids should be sharing the load…," "In my opinion, kids should be sharing the load…." All of those sound good to me, but I think I'll use "In my opinion." I like the way it sounds, and I think it will alert my reader that I am about to give my opinion.

Reflection: Let's read what I've written so far. Did you notice how I introduced the topic and then gave my opinion? I think these sentences will prepare my reader and encourage him or her to keep reading what I have to say about this topic. When you are writing an opinion, it's a good idea to introduce your topic and then clearly state your opinion. You might use a question, an example, or even a personal story to introduce the topic. As you work on your own opinion pieces today, use our chart to help you craft your sentences. Try experimenting with others too! Let's begin!

Modeled writing

Sweeping, mopping, and scrubbing the toilet—these are just a few of the many tasks that need to be done to keep the house clean. In my opinion, kids should be sharing the load and doing some of these household chores each week.

Sentence Starters for Opinion Writing:

Everyone should…	I think…
I believe…	In my opinion…
I feel…	The best thing about…
I prefer…	The worst thing about…
I strongly believe that…	If you like _____, then you will like _____ because…

Grades: 2–3

TEXT TYPE: Informative/Explanatory
LESSON FOCUS: Include Visuals to Aid Comprehension

Before the lesson, gather a few quality nonfiction books that contain strong visuals. Possible mentor texts might include the following, published by Capstone:

What Is a Plant? by Louise and Richard Spilsbury

Rain Forest Life by Janine Scott

Landforms by Jane Penrose

Also, in advance of the lesson, create a list of visuals that writers use (as shown on pages 102–105). Or invite students to identify visuals in the books they are reading and create the list with students.

STEP 1: Display a short section of your writing. Model how you reread it and think about adding a visual. Examine a mentor text and think about other possible visuals.

Think-aloud: I've been writing an informational piece about the planet Saturn. This section is about the rings of Saturn. I'm thinking I could add a visual here to help my reader understand Saturn's rings. Let's see what visuals this author included to teach the reader more or to make the piece more interesting. (Examine diagrams, illustrations, and photographs and labels from mentor texts.)

Partner talk: Now that we've looked at different kinds of visuals, which one do you think would work best for this portion of my writing?

STEP 2: Model how you create an illustration with labels.

Think-aloud: I heard some great ideas! Here's what I'm thinking: This author used an illustration with labels. Perhaps I could add an illustration with labels to my piece. It could show all of the different substances that make up the rings of Saturn. Watch as I draw a picture of Saturn and its rings. Now, I'll add some labels to make my picture clear. Watch as I write "rock, ice, and dust" and then make an arrow from the words to the picture of the rings.

Partner talk: Think together. How did adding the visual improve my writing? Is there anything you would add to make it better?

STEP 3: Reread and reflect.

Think-aloud: Listen as I reread this section of my writing and examine the visual. (After reading) I think the picture makes this section clearer and helps my reader to better understand what I've written.

Reflection: Today I showed you how writers add visuals to their nonfiction writing and how these visuals can help the reader understand more about a topic. Sometimes a good visual is worth a thousand words! It makes the writing more interesting too!

Here are other kinds of visuals that authors use when creating an informative piece of writing. (Show pages 102–105.) As you work on your writing, think about adding some visuals to make your writing more informative and interesting.

Modeled writing

Jupiter, Saturn, Uranus, and Neptune all have rings, but Saturn's rings are the only ones that can be seen through a small telescope from Earth. The rings may look solid, but they are actually made up of bits of rock, ice, and dust.

rock, ice, and dust

Types of Visuals That Writers Use

Photographs with captions

from *Ocean Craft* by Wendy Graham

Cutaway diagrams

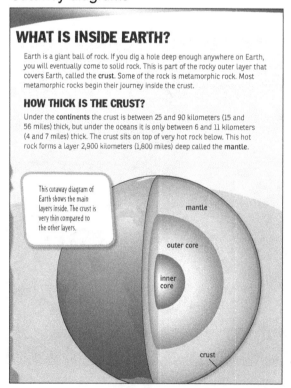

from *Metamorphic Rocks* by Chris Oxlade

Tables

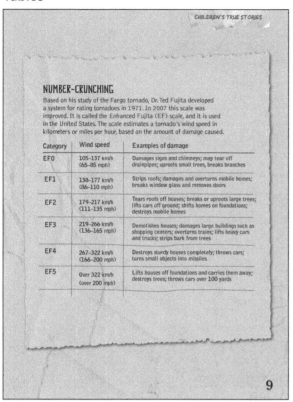

NUMBER-CRUNCHING

Based on his study of the Fargo tornado, Dr. Ted Fujita developed a system for rating tornadoes in 1971. In 2007 this scale was improved. It is called the Enhanced Fujita (EF) scale, and it is used in the United States. The scale estimates a tornado's wind speed in kilometers or miles per hour, based on the amount of damage caused.

Category	Wind speed	Examples of damage
EF0	105–137 km/h (65–85 mph)	Damages signs and chimneys; may tear off drainpipes; uproots small trees, breaks branches
EF1	138–177 km/h (86–110 mph)	Strips roofs; damages and overturns mobile homes; breaks window glass and removes doors
EF2	179–217 km/h (111–135 mph)	Tears roofs off houses; breaks or uproots large trees; lifts cars off ground; shifts homes on foundations; destroys mobile homes
EF3	219–266 km/h (136–165 mph)	Demolishes houses; damages large buildings such as shopping centers; overturns trains; lifts heavy cars and trucks; strips bark from trees
EF4	267–322 km/h (166–200 mph)	Destroys sturdy houses completely; throws cars; turns small objects into missiles
EF5	Over 322 km/h (over 200 mph)	Lifts houses off foundations and carries them away; destroys trees; throws cars over 100 yards

9

from *Surviving Tornadoes* by Elizabeth Raum

Charts

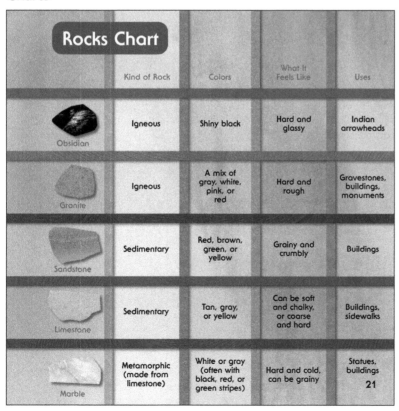

Rocks Chart

	Kind of Rock	Colors	What It Feels Like	Uses
Obsidian	Igneous	Shiny black	Hard and glassy	Indian arrowheads
Granite	Igneous	A mix of gray, white, pink, or red	Hard and rough	Gravestones, buildings, monuments
Sandstone	Sedimentary	Red, brown, green, or yellow	Grainy and crumbly	Buildings
Limestone	Sedimentary	Tan, gray, or yellow	Can be soft and chalky, or coarse and hard	Buildings, sidewalks
Marble	Metamorphic (made from limestone)	White or gray (often with black, red, or green stripes)	Hard and cold, can be grainy	Statues, buildings 21

from *Rocks: Hard, Soft, Smooth, and Rough* by Natalie Rosinsky

Diagrams

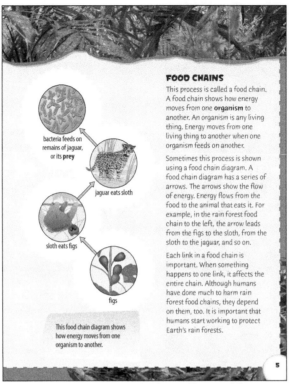

from *Rain Forest Food Chains* by Heidi Moore

Maps

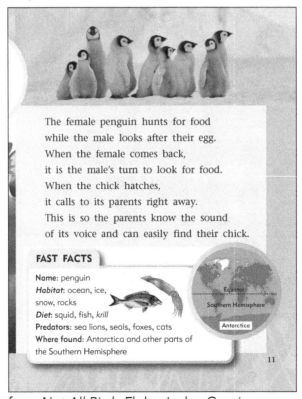

from *Not All Birds Fly* by Jaclyn Crupi

Enlargements

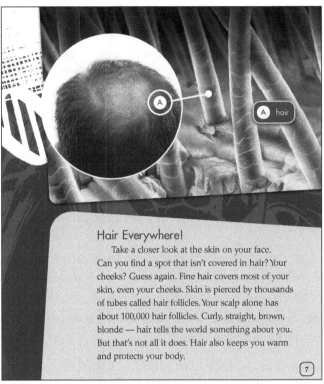

Hair Everywhere!

Take a closer look at the skin on your face. Can you find a spot that isn't covered in hair? Your cheeks? Guess again. Fine hair covers most of your skin, even your cheeks. Skin is pierced by thousands of tubes called hair follicles. Your scalp alone has about 100,000 hair follicles. Curly, straight, brown, blonde — hair tells the world something about you. But that's not all it does. Hair also keeps you warm and protects your body.

from *The Human Head* by Kathy Allen

Graphs

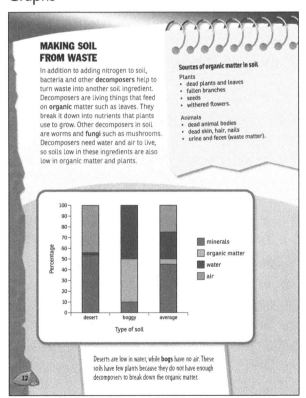

MAKING SOIL FROM WASTE

In addition to adding nitrogen to soil, bacteria and other **decomposers** help to turn waste into another soil ingredient. Decomposers are living things that feed on **organic** matter such as leaves. They break it down into nutrients that plants use to grow. Other decomposers in soil are worms and **fungi** such as mushrooms. Decomposers need water and air to live, so soils low in these ingredients are also low in organic matter and plants.

Sources of organic matter in soil

Plants
- dead plants and leaves
- fallen branches
- seeds
- withered flowers.

Animals
- dead animal bodies
- dead skin, hair, nails
- urine and feces (waste matter).

Deserts are low in water, while **bogs** have no air. These soils have few plants because they do not have enough decomposers to break down the organic matter.

from *Soil* by Richard and Louise Spilsbury

Grades: 2–3

TEXT TYPE: Personal Narrative
LESSON FOCUS: Use Temporal Words to Signal Event Order

In advance of the lesson, create a chart like the one shown on page 107. It lists temporal words and phrases that show sequence or order. Or invite students to identify temporal words in the books they are reading and create the chart *with* students.

STEP 1: Use words from the chart to talk about a familiar event.

> *Think-aloud: Temporal words are words that show order or sequence. Writers use them to help readers understand the order of events in a piece of writing. Let's think back to yesterday's Fun Run at our school. Listen as I use words from the chart to tell about it. I'll point to a temporal word or phrase each time I use one.*
>
> *First, we put on our running shoes and grabbed our water bottles. Then, we went outside to the starting line. We stretched and warmed up by doing some jumping jacks. As soon as Mrs. Navas blew her whistle, we all began to run. After we ran many laps, we collapsed in a tired heap. At last, we were given some water and healthy snacks.*
>
> *Partner talk: Your turn! Think about the fire drill we had last week. Tell your partner about it, using as many temporal words from our chart as you can.*

STEP 2: Model how you infuse temporal words and phrases as you write.

> *Think-aloud: As writers, we can use these temporal words when we write too! I'm writing about the first time I hiked to Grotto Falls. As I think back to that day, I remember that I could hear the waterfall before I saw it. I think I'll write, "During the last half-mile of the hike, I could hear the rushing waters of the falls, and I knew that I must be getting close." The word "during" will help my reader understand the order of things. (Continue writing, modeling how you include temporal words to signal order.)*
>
> *Partner talk: Talk with your partner. What other words or phrases could I use with these sentences?*

STEP 3: Continue writing, thinking aloud about the temporal words you can infuse.

Think-aloud: I remember that I was so mesmerized by the beauty of the waterfall, I simply stood there for a moment and didn't say a word. I think I'll start my next sentence with the phrase "for a moment." Let me say it out loud and listen to how it sounds: "<u>For a moment</u>, I didn't move or speak. I simply stared and listened." I like the way that sounds, and I think the phrase "for a moment" will make it clear to my reader that it took me a moment to say anything.

Reflection: Writers, today I showed you how I use temporal words to help my reader understand the order of events in my piece. You watched as I carefully chose words that would help make the sequence of my narrative clear.

As you work on your own piece of writing today, use our chart to choose words that show the order in which things happen. You might think of some other words that aren't on our chart. You can experiment with those too!

Modeled writing

<u>During</u> the last half-mile of the hike, I could hear the rushing waters of the falls, and I knew that I must be getting close. I quickened my pace, anxious to see the waterfall that so many of my friends had talked about. <u>After a while</u>, I turned a corner and found myself face to face with a mass of rushing and falling water. <u>For a moment</u>, I didn't move or speak. I simply stared and listened. Grotto Falls was living up to its reputation. It was mesmerizing.

Temporal Words and Phrases:

after	as soon as	first	not long after
after a long time	at last	for a moment	shortly
after a while	before	last	soon after
after that	during	later	then
afterward	finally	next	

Grades: 4–5

TEXT TYPE: Opinion

LESSON FOCUS: Link Opinion and Reasons Using Words, Phrases, and Clauses

In advance of the lesson, create a chart like the one shown on page 109 that lists linking words. Or, invite students to identify linking words in the books they are reading and create the chart *with* students.

STEP 1: Think aloud as you consider words from the chart to craft your opinion.

Think-aloud: Linking words, phrases, and clauses join one idea to the next. When we are giving an opinion, we can use linking words to connect our opinion with the reasons that support our opinion. These words strengthen our writing and cause the reader to think more deeply about our topic.

I am crafting a letter to the chamber of commerce, asking the members to consider building a new aquatic center for our town. Watch me as I use words from this chart to help me as I write. First, I'll write my opinion. I'll write, "I think our town needs a new aquatic center." I think our current pool is old, so I'll write: "The pool near Bogert Park is old and run down." I want to explain that because it's old, it's often closed during the summer for repairs. I could say, "Consequently, it's often closed…." Or I could say, "Therefore, it's often closed…."

Partner talk: What other words or phrases could I use to link my opinion and reason? Talk them over with your partner.

STEP 2: Begin writing, thinking aloud about the linking words you can use.

Think-aloud: Sometimes, it's helpful to say the sentence out loud when I'm writing. That way, I can hear what it would sound like to a reader. I think I'll say: "As a result, it's often closed for repairs, leaving no public pool for people to enjoy on hot summer days." I think "as a result" is a good linking word to use here. It's clear, and it links my opinion and reason nicely.

I also want to say that because it's old, it uses a lot more water than the newer pools use. So I'll need another linking word here.

Partner talk: Think together. What word from our chart could I use?

STEP 3: Continue writing and thinking aloud.

Think-aloud: I think the word "furthermore" would be good here. Watch me as I write my next sentence. "Furthermore, the current pool requires much more water than newer, more modern pools. So it's wasting our town's precious water!" Let's reread what I've written so far and see how it sounds. (After rereading) I think these linking words strengthen my argument and make my writing sound more polished and convincing.

Reflection: Today I showed you how I link my opinion and reasons using words, clauses, and phrases. You observed me as I carefully chose words or phrases that sounded good and strengthened my opinion. As you write today, use our chart to help you choose words or phrases to link your opinion and reasons. You might think of words that aren't on our chart. You can experiment with those too!

Modeled writing

I think our town needs a new aquatic center. The pool near Bogert Park is old and run down. <u>As a result</u>, it's often closed for repairs, leaving no public pool for people to enjoy on hot summer days. <u>Furthermore</u>, the current pool requires much more water than newer, more modern pools. So it's wasting our town's precious water!

Linking Words for Opinion Writing:

additionally	for example	in fact	specifically
another point	for instance	in order to	therefore
as a result	furthermore	in particular	
consequently	in addition	moreover	

Grades: 4–5

TEXT TYPE: Informative/Explanatory

LESSON FOCUS: Use Headings to Group Related Information

Before the lesson, gather a few quality nonfiction books that contain headings. Possible mentor texts might include the following, published by Capstone:

What Is a Landform? by Rebecca Rissman

Mountain Tops by Ellen Labrecque

Peculiar Plants by Anita Ganeri

In advance of the lesson, create a chart like the one shown on page 111 that identifies three different types of headings. Or invite students to examine the headings found in the nonfiction books they are reading and create the chart with students.

STEP 1: Examine a mentor text and think about how the author used headings.

Think-aloud: As we read nonfiction texts, we often see headings. As readers, headings help us understand what each section of text is about. In the book Mountain Tops, *the author used a variety of headings. She placed the headings in a prominent place on the page and made them using a larger font. The heading on this page is "Dangerous Mountains." When I see that heading, I know that the information on this page will tell me about some of the world's most dangerous mountains. On this page, the author used a question as a heading: "Why Are Mountain Tops Unexplored?"*

Partner talk: Think together. Why else would an author include headings in his or her writing? How do headings help the reader?

STEP 2: Think aloud as you create a heading for a section of writing.

Think-aloud: I'm working on a piece about glaciers, and I need to create a heading for this section that explains why glaciers sometimes look blue. I noticed in our mentor text that a heading can be represented with a word, a phrase, or even a question. I could use the heading "Why Are Glaciers Blue?" That would alert my reader that I am about to explain why glaciers sometimes look blue. Another idea for a heading could be "Blue Ice."

Partner talk: Put your heads together. What other headings could I use for this section?

STEP 3: Choose a heading. Then reread and reflect.

Think-aloud: I'm thinking I'll use "Blue Ice" for this heading. I think it might offer some intrigue for my reader because we usually think of ice as clear or white. I also like this heading because it sums up what this section is about. Now listen as I read my heading and this section of writing to see how it works. I think this heading works well!

Reflection: Headings tell a reader exactly what to expect from a section of writing. Today, you observed as I thought about a heading I could use in my writing. I examined what another writer did, and it helped me to think about my own work. As you craft your own piece of writing today, try to include some headings to help your reader more easily navigate your text.

Modeled writing

Blue Ice
Look closely at the ice that makes up a glacier and you might notice that it looks blue, but it's not. The glacial ice simply looks blue because it is so thick and compressed that it absorbs every other color in the color spectrum.

Type of heading	What it is	Example
topic heading	a heading that is a word or short phrase	*Prickly Plants*
statement heading	a heading that uses both a noun and verb	*A Plant That Eats Meat*
question heading	a heading that is in the form of a question	*What Are Peculiar Plants?*

Grades: 4–5

TEXT TYPE: Personal Narrative

LESSON FOCUS: Use Dialogue to Develop Experiences and Events

STEP 1: Construct a short piece of writing without dialogue.

Think-aloud: I've been working on a narrative about the time my sister and I had a camping adventure. I'm working on the section of writing where we realize we had forgotten to pack the tent. (See "First draft" on page 113.) As I reread this, I'm thinking it's okay, but I think adding some dialogue would make this a lot more interesting. Dialogue does that. It draws your reader into the setting and makes a reader feel as if he or she is right there with you.

Partner talk: Put your heads together. What dialogue could I add to this section of my piece?

STEP 2: Think aloud as you construct the piece of writing using dialogue.

Think-aloud: This time, I'm going to add some dialogue to make my writing come to life. I think the first two sentences are okay, so I'm going to leave those as they are. I think I could add some dialogue with the next sentence. I remember that I told my sister I would start working on the tent. I'll write: "I'll start working on the tent." Now, I could write, "I said," but I think it would be more interesting if I wrote: "I shouted over my shoulder as I headed back to the car for another load." Did you notice how I put quotation marks around the words that I spoke? I also added a comma after those words and before "I shouted...." That's important to remember when you add dialogue.

Partner talk: What do you think of my second draft so far? Do you think the dialogue helps? Why or why not?

STEP 3: Continue to think aloud as you write.

Think-aloud: I remember that my sister simply said, "The tent..." as if she was thinking about it. Her voice kind of trailed off when she said it. So, I think I'll write: "My sister looked up from her task, a strange look on her face. 'The tent...,' she said, her voice trailing."

I'll keep going with the dialogue here. I remember asking her if she packed it and, at this point, I was beginning to feel a little nervous. I think I'll say: "'You packed the tent, didn't you?'" Here, I think I'll use "I said," but I'll add a comma and tell my reader I was beginning to feel anxious. I think I'll add one more piece of dialogue here. I remember that my sister just stared at me and said, "Um…." That's when I knew for sure we had forgotten the tent. Watch as I get that piece of dialogue down on the page.

Reflection: *Today I showed you how writers infuse dialogue into their writing. Let's reread both of my drafts. I think the second draft is much better than the first, don't you? Dialogue, when it's used well, can enrich a piece of writing and make it more interesting. As you work on your own piece of narrative writing today, try to infuse some dialogue and see what you think. I think you'll like what it does to the writing!*

Modeled writing

First draft:
Excitedly, we began to unpack the car and set up camp. My sister gathered wood and started making a small fire. I offered to start working on the tent. My sister looked at me with a strange look on her face. I began to wonder where the tent was. I hadn't seen it when I unloaded the car. I couldn't believe it! We had forgotten the tent!

Second draft:
Excitedly, we began to unpack the car and set up camp. My sister gathered wood and started making a small fire.

"I'll start working on the tent," I shouted over my shoulder as I headed back to the car for another load.

My sister looked up from her task, a strange look on her face. "The tent…" she said, her voice trailing.

"You packed the tent, didn't you?" I said, starting to feel a twinge of anxiety.

"Um…" was all she could muster.

That was all I needed to hear. It was clear. We had driven all this way to go camping… but without a tent.

Chapter 8:

TRANSFORMATIONS

"Children will continually surprise us if we let them."

— Donald Graves

Below are two different writing samples from a first-grade student. The first piece, written in September, shows a self-portrait: "My Body." The student has drawn a picture and included several labels, such as *hair, hand, head, shoulders, leg, shoe, knee,* and *toe.*

The second sample shows a piece of writing that was crafted by the same student in April.

September

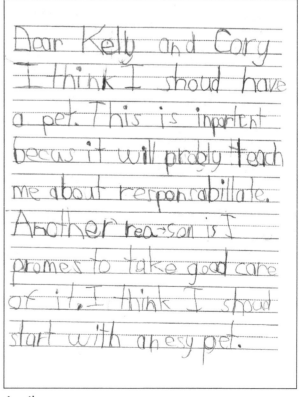

April

I think it's fair to say that this student has grown as a writer. In fact, in my opinion, there's been a dramatic change in this writer's capabilities.

Look again at the two writing samples. What can you infer about the writing instruction in this classroom? What kinds of things might have taken place in this classroom to bring about the transformation in this child's writing ability?

As I examine both pieces of writing, there are a couple of things I can infer:

Writing happened every day.

- Students become better writers by *writing*. It's clear to me that this teacher valued writing; therefore, she made writing instruction a priority. Rather than simply sprinkling writing throughout the instructional day, she provided large chunks of time for her students to engage in writing each day.

The teacher modeled—a lot.

- I can infer that the teacher in this first-grade classroom thought out loud and wrote in front of her students often. She demonstrated what writers do before they write, while they are writing, and when they are finished writing.

Throughout this book, I've argued that modeling has the power to transform the writing classroom. Some of you, as you read the previous chapters, may have been thinking: *Sure, modeling is a nifty way to teach writing, but can it truly transform the writing classroom? Can it really make a difference in the kind of writing my students produce?*

The short answer to both of these questions is "yes."

Webster's Dictionary defines "transformation" as "a thorough or dramatic change." When we make our thinking and writing public, when we invite our students to bear witness to our own writing process, we will begin to see dramatic improvement in our students' writing.

On the next few pages, we'll examine the work of three different students. The students are all in different grades and live in different states. But they have one thing in common: They had the opportunity to hear a teacher's thinking and see a teacher's writing. As you consider each piece of writing, I think you'll agree that modeling is the key that unlocks a world of potential for our students and their writing.

September

Madison, like most emergent writers, has conveyed her writing mostly through her picture. She's included enough detail in the picture to engage a reader, and she's included a couple of letters.

February

Madison has now added words to help her reader know even more about her topic. Her writing is readable and shows a growing knowledge of letter and sound relationships. In addition, she's added a second sentence that provides more details about the zebra. In four short months, her writing ability has made a huge leap!

Madison's teacher most likely has modeled her own thinking and writing, demonstrating how she chooses a topic, plans for her writing, and uses letters and words to communicate with a reader.

GRADE 1

September

Kylie starts the school year with some solid writing skills. Her writing is readable, and her picture and text go together. However, there's not much writing on the page, and the details of the camping trip are completely missing. Kylie, like most first-grade writers, writes one sentence and is done.

March

By March, Kylie's writing has blossomed! She utilizes some transition words that keep her piece clear and organized, and she includes details she omitted in her writing in September. She also creates a strong and satisfying conclusion: "All in all, Utah was great."

GRADE 4

September

In September, Clark's teacher asked her students to write about something that helps them to recall memories. Clark writes about his "camo" bracelet, and he has a lot to say, but the writing lacks clarity, focus, and voice.

> Clark, fourth grade
>
> My one thing that reminds me of a memory is my camo bracelet that I made. I learned to make them at a play date I had at Cade's house. Once Cade's mom taught me how to make them we made bracelets the whole time. The bracelets are made out of 550 survival cord. About a day later I got some survival cord and made a camo bracelet. This camo bracelet reminds me of Mrs. Shaw because Mrs. Shaw made our class write notes to the army and navy and the army uses camo a lot. So that's why my camo bracelet reminded me of Mrs. Shaw.

April

> Clark, fourth grade
>
> #### C.S. Lewis
>
> Did you know the book: The Lion, The Witch, and The Wardrobe was inspired by C.S. Lewis' life and faith?
>
> I think you should vote for C.S. Lewis as the Grand Marshall for three amazing reasons.
>
> The first reason you should vote for C.S. Lewis, or "Jack" as everyone called him, is because he was highly imaginative. For instance, Jack and his older brother Warren played in their attic for hours and hours creating new worlds. One world Jack created was called Animal Land which showed Jack's love for animals and that's why there are so many animals in the *Chronicles of Narnia*.
>
> The second reason you should vote for C.S. Lewis for the Grand Marshall is because he was such a great writer. Jack was such a great writer because he wrote every single day. In his lifetime, Jack wrote over 100 books and poems. He was extremely talented with his word choice and his words took the reader on an imaginary adventure. By far, *The Lion, the Witch, and the Wardrobe* is the most popular of all his books.
>
> The third reason that you should vote for C.S. Lewis for Grand Marshall is that he was extremely generous. For example, Jack fought in World War 1, where he made a promise to a friend named Paddy that if one of them died, and the other survived, they would care for the other's family. Sadly, Paddy was killed in the war and Jack survived. So he kept his promise and cared for Paddy's mother and sister for the rest of their lives.
>
> Surely you can see that C.S. Lewis was a great man because of his incredible imagination. He was also a world-changing writer, and he was willing to give up his life for others. Without a doubt, I think you should vote for C.S. Lewis as the Grand Marshall.

In April, Clark's teacher announced that the class would be creating a Personality Parade. Each student was asked to choose a famous person that they admire, research, and then write a persuasive piece explaining why that person should be chosen as the "Grand Marshall of the Personality Parade."

Clark's persuasive piece is clear and organized. He incorporates many of the skills that were likely modeled in his teacher's mini-lessons, including:

- Use of transitional words and phrases,
- Backing up your opinion with evidence, and
- Varying sentence beginnings.

Clark has shown tremendous growth in just six months!

When you look at these writing samples and the growth that each writer made, it's easy to see why I believe modeling is so powerful. Through teacher modeling, students are given a vision of who they could be as writers. As they observe another teacher think, plan, make decisions, write, revise, edit, and publish, they learn that the writing process is a process of discovery. They see what's possible in their own writing, and they are assured that their teacher will serve as a guide each step of the way. They are…transformed.

Chapter 9:

WORK WORTH DOING

"Far and away the best prize that life offers is the chance
to work hard at work worth doing."

— Theodore Roosevelt

Nearly 20 years ago, when I began my first teaching assignment in a first-grade classroom, I knew in my heart that writing was something I needed to teach, but I didn't have the faintest idea how to go about it. So each day during writing time, I passed out a "story starter." It was a sheet of paper with a writing prompt at the top. For example, it might say: *One morning I woke up as a squirrel. I….* Following the prompt, there were lines on which students could write.

Each day, I would read the story starter out loud to my class and then say something like: *Okay, so think about what it would be like if you woke up and realized that you were a squirrel. Use these lines to write about what you would do.*

Then I would send my students off to write.

As you can imagine, what proceeded was a management nightmare. As emergent writers, my students were just beginning to use letters to represent sounds, and many of them lacked the confidence, skills, and stamina to write independently. Most of my students sat for long periods of time, hands waving in the air, waiting for me to come and help them. Other students had simply given up altogether and were sharpening and re-sharpening their pencils or playing with the items in their desks. It was clear to me (and to anyone visiting my classroom) that I was in over my head.

As I think back to that first year of teaching, I realize that I was doing the best I could with the skills I had. There were no writing methods courses in college that prepared me to teach writing. I knew enough to structure a time each day for students to write, but I had no idea how to use that time to *teach* my students how to write.

My principal, sensing that I needed some support, gave me two precious gifts: First, she sent me to a workshop focused on writing instruction. And, second, she covered my class so that I could observe another teacher in my building teach writing.

I took copious notes at the conference, and my mind swirled with research, skills, teaching tools, and ideas. And when I watched a more experienced colleague put these things into practice, *modeling* what good writing instruction looks like and sounds like, my teaching began to change dramatically.

Hungry for more, I pored over professional books about writing instruction. I signed up for after-school sessions focused on writing, and I began to have more and more conversations about writing with teachers in my school. Inspired by what I read and saw and heard, I tried new things. My lessons were less than perfect, and sometimes they simply…flopped. But I brushed myself off, gained some valuable insights, and tried again.

I ditched the "story starters" and, instead, invited my students to write about what they *knew* about and what they *cared* about. I encouraged them to examine the work of famous authors and to write for actual readers.

And, I modeled.

Each day, I made my thinking visible as I crafted my own piece of writing. Mesmerized, my students watched my marker move across the page. They observed me as I used pictures and letters and words and sentences to say something meaningful to my reader.

I noticed that everything improved when I took the time to explicitly model my own thinking and writing. Over time, I noticed that my students:

- were more motivated to write,

- tackled the courageous work of revision with greater enthusiasm,

- were more willing to take risks with their writing,

- asked to write when it wasn't writing time,

- wrote voluntarily at home,

- saw themselves as capable and developing writers, and

- rarely uttered the once-dreaded words: "I don't know what to write about!"

I think you'll find that the being-a-writer will teach you how to be a writer (and a teacher of writing).

My modeling and the writing my students were producing were not perfect, but it was clear that we were all growing as writers. During writing time, the classroom hummed with activity and conversation, exploration and excitement.

I'm still learning and evolving as a writer and a teacher of writing. This book represents my current thinking about writing and writing instruction. Like students, my thinking changes and evolves as I work with student writers, read, wonder, think, and engage in conversations with other teachers.

Thomas Newkirk (2013) spoke to a group of educators who were gathered for a conference in Boston. His words are an invitation to you and to me.

"…I think as you move into big projects there's always a feeling that you need to be ready before you can start, right? Well, I think you're never ready. I think one of the things about the writing process that you learn is that the process, itself, teaches you how to do the project. You're never ready to be a parent. You're never ready to be a husband. You're never ready. But I know with my daughter—my daughter taught me how to be a parent. The being-a-parent taught me how to be a parent. The diving into a project teaches you how to do the project."

Engaging in modeled writing might feel like an enormous leap for you. It may feel strange and uncomfortable to put yourself, your thinking, and your writing "out there" for the world to see—even if the "world" consists only of the four walls of your classroom.

It's true that you might not feel ready. But please don't wait until you do. If you dive in and begin to make your thinking and writing transparent for students, I think you'll be surprised at what you discover. I think you'll find that the being-a-writer will teach you how to be a writer (and a teacher of writing). And I think you'll discover that, though teaching writing well is hard, it is work worth doing.

APPENDIX

On the pages that follow are samples and reproducibles that can be used when planning for modeled writing and working with student writers.

I've included several different samples and reproducibles that can be used to plan units that span several weeks or to plan mini-lessons for individual days. For each sample, you will find a brief explanation and an example of how I might use it in the classroom. The blank reproducibles can be copied for use in your classroom.

Teachers often ask me if I think of, plan for, or write out my modeled writing before I write in front of my students. I don't. In my opinion, it's much more authentic if my writing piece is created "on the spot." In other words, if I do all of the hard work of thinking and writing, crossing out, and starting over before I write in front of students, then they aren't really getting an authentic view of writing. So as you examine the planning templates, you'll notice there isn't a place for you to plan out and write your modeled writing. My hope is that you'll do that in front of your students.

However, if you're new to modeled writing, it's perfectly okay to do a little thinking and planning before you model. Some teachers find it helpful to jot down their ideas (or their brief piece of writing) on a sticky note. They place the sticky note in an inconspicuous place so that they can refer to it when they are modeling. It's a scaffold that may help you when you first begin writing in front of your students, but remember that scaffolds are temporary supports and should eventually be removed. I encourage you, at some point, to leave the sticky note behind and let your students see your authentic thinking and writing, even if it's not perfect.

Sample Genre Study Planning

GENRE: Personal Narrative   **GRADE:** 3

 # OF WEEKS: 3 weeks

Mini-lesson Topics:	Primary Goals:
• We all have stories to tell (listen to and tell stories from our lives—create a topics list) • Examining mentor texts for structure of personal narrative • Features of a strong personal narrative (create anchor chart) • Using sketches to plan for writing (stretching out a brief moment in time) • Thinking about audience • Crafting an inviting lead (revisit mentor texts) • Rereading as you write with an eye for organization and structure • Using temporal words to signal event order and keep a piece organized • Creating a satisfying conclusion	• Organization and structure • Rereading • Conclusion
	Secondary Goals:
	• Temporal words • Rereading to revise as I go
	Resources/Materials:

	Mentor texts:
	  My Name Is Yoon by Helen Recorvits
	  All the Places to Love by Patricia MacLachlan
	Anchor charts:
	  • Features of a personal narrative
	  • Sketching to plan for writing
	  • Temporal words

Reflections:	**Learning Targets:**
Keep writers on track with audience and purpose. For whom are you writing this?	CCSS.ELA-LITERACY.W.3.3.A CCSS.ELA-LITERACY.W.3.3.C CCSS.ELA-LITERACY.W.3.3.D CCSS.ELA-LITERACY.W.3.4

This template allows you to plan for an entire unit that is focused on a particular genre. In addition to the spaces to record mini-lesson topics, learning goals, materials, and learning targets, there is a space for you to jot down thoughts and reflections during and after the unit. These reflections will help you the next time you teach a unit on the same genre.

Sample Mentors and Modeling Planning

GENRE STUDY: Informative

Mentor Text(s)	Writing Skill	Teaching Move(s)
Amazing Military Robots by Sean Stewart Price *Body Bugs: Invisible Creatures Lurking Inside You* by Jennifer Swanson	strong leads	• Invite pairs to examine leads found in other nonfiction books and look for "leads we love." • Record leads on an anchor chart. • Model how to use the chart when crafting a lead.
Not All Birds Fly by Jaclyn Crupi	diagrams	Model how I include a diagram in my piece about Saturn.
Animal Spikes and Spines by Rebecca Rissman	bold words	Using my piece about Saturn, model how I choose which words to write in boldface.

With careful thought and planning, mentor texts and modeling prove to be a powerful combination. This planning template allows you to list the mentor texts that you plan to use for a particular genre study. Once the titles are listed, you can record the skill that will be taught through examination of the text. You can list your specific teaching moves in the third column.

Many teachers share these planning templates with the school librarian or media specialist so that the books can be ordered or gathered prior to teaching the writing unit.

Sample Mini-lesson Planning

DATE: 3/14

Mini-lesson Planning	
Lesson focus	Using temporal words to signal event order
Why? *Students learn why today's skill is important to them as writers and how the lesson relates to the work they are doing.*	Temporal words are words that show order or sequence. Writers use them to help readers understand the order of events in a piece of writing. It keeps our personal narratives organized and easy to understand.
Materials needed	Anchor chart with list of temporal words
Possible modeled writing topic	Continue my narrative about hiking to Hidden Lake
Questions for partner talk	What other words or phrases could I have used with these sentences? What do you think about my piece of writing now? Did adding the temporal words improve my narrative?
Anchor chart created	Yes √ No
Question(s) for reflection	What words or phrases did you include in your narrative today? Do you think it improved your piece of writing? Why or why not?

This daily planning template can be used to record your thinking and your teaching moves so that your mini-lesson can be brief and focused. When we give careful consideration to each portion of our lesson, we will be able to maximize our teaching and students will learn more.

Sample Mini-lesson Planning 2

DATE: 5/12

Component	Time	Teaching Move(s)
Focused mini-lesson Think aloud, write, explicitly teach Set the stage for writing	8–10 minutes	• Introduce the topic and state an opinion • Model using my own opinion piece about kids and chores • Anchor chart: Sentence Starters for Opinion Writing
Independent writing Students write Teacher coaches and confers	20–40 minutes	**Conferred with:** Jacob Lin Grace Ella Nikil
Reflection Gather students and reflect: • What did I learn about myself as a writer? • What new strategy did I try and how did it work? • How can I use what I learned to help me as a writer?	3–5 minutes	Who used our chart to help them write today? Share the first few sentences of your piece with your partner.

This is another version of a template that can be used to plan your daily mini-lesson. It's organized by the components of the writing block and includes a space for you to record the names of students that you conferred with. There may be times when I think: *I need to check in with Ella today,* but I typically don't plan which students I will confer with each day. Instead, I prefer to record the names of the students that I actually conferred with that day.

Sample Weekly Mini-lesson Planning

WEEK OF: September 22–26
GENRE: Personal Narrative

	Lesson Focus	Materials	Conferred with:
Monday	Using sketches to plan for writing (stretching out a brief moment in time)	Anchor chart: Sketches Help Us Plan Our Writing	Grayson Ally Kendra Will Ivy Olivia
Tuesday	Crafting an inviting lead	Mentor texts Anchor chart: Leads We Love	Hailey Elena Aman Kaden
Wednesday	Using temporal words to signal event order	Anchor chart: Temporal Words	Madison Clark Lee Nora Ian
Thursday	Rereading as you write with an eye for organization and structure	My own modeled writing piece	Eric Jamal Cooper Lilly
Friday	Crafting a satisfying ending	Mentor texts Anchor chart: Different Kinds of Endings	Judah Tara Ella Ryder

If you prefer to see a week's worth of mini-lessons at one glance, this weekly planning template might work best for you. The specific focus for each day's lesson is listed, along with any materials that will be needed. There's also a column to record the names of the students that you conferred with on that day.

Sample Weekly Mini-lesson Planning 2

WEEK OF: November 3–8

GENRE: Personal Narrative

Component	Time	Monday	Tuesday	Wednesday	Thursday	Friday
Focused mini-lesson: Think aloud, write, explicitly teach Set the stage for writing	8–10 min.	Using sketches to plan for writing (stretching out a brief moment in time) Make Anchor chart	Crafting an inviting lead Mentor texts Anchor chart: Leads We Love	Using temporal words to signal event order Anchor chart: Temporal Words	Rereading as you write with an eye for organization and structure	Crafting a satisfying conclusion Mentor texts: ways that authors conclude
Independent writing: Students write Teacher coaches and confers	20–40 min.	Conferred with: Grayson Will Ally Olivia Kendra Ivy	Conferred with: Hailey Elena Aman Kaden	Conferred with: Madison Clark Lee Nora Ian	Conferred with: Eric Jamal Cooper Lilly	Conferred with: Judah Tara Ella Ryder
Reflection: Gather students and reflect: • What did I learn about myself as a writer? • What new strategy did I try and how did it work? • How can I use what I learned to help me as a writer?	3–5 min.	Did making and using the sketches help you as you wrote? Why or why not?	What kinds of leads did you try for your narrative? How do you feel about the lead you chose?	Who used some temporal words from our chart today?	Did anyone make changes to their piece when they stopped to reread? What did you notice about rereading?	Share your conclusion with your partner. What do you think?

This version of a weekly planning template uses the components of the daily writing block to help focus your thinking and planning. The first row provides a space for you to record the focus of each day's mini-lesson, along with any materials that are needed for the lesson. During each day's independent writing time, you can jot down the names of the students with whom you conferred. Finally, there's a space allotted for you to plan for the kinds of questions you will ask when your students gather to reflect on the day's writing.

Sample Conference Record Sheet (Primary)

WRITER: Jacob

Date	I can...	I'm working on...
9/12	draw a picture to tell my story.	adding words to my picture.
9/19	add labels to my picture.	using the alphabet card to help me write words.

This simple conference record sheet can be used to keep track of what you notice as you confer with individual writers. As you confer, carefully notice and note what you see the writer doing well. For example, you might say: *Wow! I see that you have a detailed picture here. It tells me, as the reader, so much about your story. I'm going to write that down in the "I can..." column. Now it says, "I can draw a picture to tell my story." That's what writers and illustrators do, isn't it?*

The last column provides a space for you to record *one* specific skill that the writer can work on moving forward. Explicitly teach the skill and demonstrate, if necessary. For example, you might say: *Can I show you something else that writers do? Writers add letters and words to their picture. When they do that, they tell their reader even more about their story. Watch me as I do that with this picture that I drew. I can write the word "me" right here next to the picture of me. That way, my reader will know that is a picture of me. And, right next to the picture of my cat, I can write "Zoe" because that's my cat's name. As you keep writing, try adding some words to your pictures. I'll jot that down in this column. Now it says, "I'm working on adding words to my picture." I'll check back with you later to see how it's going.*

If you choose, you can keep your completed record sheets in a binder, where you can access this information when you need it. However, I prefer to place these sheets in the *student's* writing folder. While it's true that *you* need to know what writers are doing well and what they need to work on next, it's even more important that *students* know these things.

Sample Conference Record Sheet (Intermediate)

WRITER: Hannah

Date	Genre	Glow...	Grow...
9/6	Personal narrative	strong and inviting lead strong sense of organization	Use varying sentence beginnings. (Stop and reread often with an eye for sentence beginnings.)
9/12	Personal narrative	good use of transition words (then, suddenly, at last...)	Try several endings out loud in order to choose one that works best.

For intermediate students, I add a column to indicate the genre of the writing they are working on. In addition, I use the terms "Glow" and "Grow" to record what I see the writer doing well and what skill the writer could focus on next. The comments that you place in the "Glow..." column should be genuine and specific so that the writer knows exactly what's working in the piece of writing. The "Grow..." column is a place to record the *one* thing you want the writer to work on moving forward. Make sure that you explicitly teach the skill during the conference so that the writer is clear about his or her goal.

If you choose, you can keep your completed record sheets in a binder, where you can access this information when you need it. However, I prefer to place these sheets in the *student's* writing folder. While it's true that *you* need to know what writers are doing well and what they need to work on next, it's even more important that *students* know these things.

Genre Study Planning Template

GENRE: _____ **GRADE:** _____

 # OF WEEKS: _____

Mini-lesson Topics:	Primary Goals:
	Secondary Goals:
	Resources/Materials:

Reflections:	Learning Targets:

Mentors and Modeling Planning Template

GENRE STUDY: _____

Mentor Text(s)	Writing Skill	Teaching Move(s)

Mini-lesson Planning Template

DATE: _____

Mini-lesson Planning	
Lesson focus	
Why? *Students learn why today's skill is important to them as writers and how the lesson relates to the work they are doing.*	
Materials needed	
Possible modeled writing topic	
Questions for partner talk	
Anchor chart created	Yes No
Question(s) for reflection	

Mini-lesson Planning 2 Template

DATE: _____

Component	Time	Teaching Move(s)
Focused mini-lesson Think aloud, write, explicitly teach Set the stage for writing	8–10 minutes	
Independent writing Students write Teacher coaches and confers	20–40 minutes	Conferred with:
Reflection Gather students and reflect: • What did I learn about myself as a writer? • What new strategy did I try and how did it work? • How can I use what I learned to help me as a writer?	3–5 minutes	

Weekly Mini-lesson Planning Template

WEEK OF: _____

GENRE: _____

	Lesson Focus	Materials	Conferred with:
Monday			
Tuesday			
Wednesday			
Thursday			
Friday			

Weekly Mini-lesson Planning 2 Template

WEEK OF: _____

GENRE: _____

Component	Time	Monday	Tuesday	Wednesday	Thursday	Friday
Focused mini-lesson: Think aloud, write, explicitly teach Set the stage for writing	8–10 min.					
Independent writing: Students write Teacher coaches and confers	20–40 min.	Conferred with:	Conferred with:	Conferred with:	Conferred with:	Conferred with:
Reflection: Gather students and reflect: • What did I learn about myself as a writer? • What new strategy did I try and how did it work? • How can I use what I learned to help me as a writer?	3–5 min.					

Conference Record Sheet (Primary)

WRITER: _____

Date	I can...	I'm working on...

Conference Record Sheet (Intermediate)

WRITER: _____

Date	Genre	Glow...	Grow...

CAPSTONE/HEINEMANN-RAINTREE REFERENCES

Amazing Military Robots by Sean Stewart Price

Amazon Adventure by Layne deMarin

And Then There Were Eight: Poems about Space by Laura Purdie Salas

Animal Spikes and Spines by Rebecca Rissman

Be the Best at Writing by Rebecca Rissman

Body Bugs: Invisible Creatures Lurking Inside You by Jennifer Swanson

Costa Rica by Elizabeth Raum

Diary of Sallie Hester: A Covered Wagon Girl by Sallie Hester

Going to School: Comparing Past and Present by Rebecca Rissman

Goodnight Baseball by Michael Dahl

Goodnight Football by Michael Dahl

How Can We Help Out in Our Community? by Tony Stead

How Much Time Should Kids Spend Online? by Tony Stead

Landforms by Jane Penrose

Lost Little Penguin by Tracey Corderoy

Metamorphic Rocks by Chris Oxlade

Mountain Tops by Ellen Labrecque

Not All Birds Fly by Jaclyn Crupi

Ocean Craft by Wendy Graham

Peculiar Plants by Anita Ganeri

Pick a Picture, Write an Opinion! by Kristen McCurry

Rain Forest Animal Adaptations by Lisa J. Amstutz

Rain Forest Food Chains by Heidi Moore

Rain Forest Life by Janine Scott

Rocks: Hard, Soft, Smooth, and Rough by Natalie Rosinsky

Should Children Have Homework? by Tony Stead

Should We Squash Bugs? by Tony Stead

Soil by Richard and Louise Spilsbury

Southeast Indians by Andrew Santella

Space by Martha E. H. Rustad

Surviving Tornadoes by Elizabeth Raum

The Human Head by Kathy Allen

Volcano Explorers by Pam Rosenberg

What Is a Landform? by Rebecca Rissman

What Is a Plant? by Louise and Richard Spilsbury

What Is the Best Pet? by Tony Stead

Whiteout!: A Book About Blizzards by Rick Thomas and Denise Shea

Why Should We Recycle? by Tony Stead

REFERENCES

Allington, Richard. "What I've Learned about Effective Reading Instruction From a Decade of Studying Exemplary Elementary Classroom Teachers." *Phi Delta Kappan* 83, no. 10 (2002): 740–47.

Anderson, Jeff. *Everyday Editing: Inviting Students to Develop Skill and Craft in Writer's Workshop.* Portland, ME: Stenhouse Publishers, 2007.

_____. *Mechanically Inclined: Building Grammar, Usage, and Style into Writer's Workshop.* Portland, ME: Stenhouse Publishers, 2005.

Applebee, A. N., J. A. Langer, M. Nystrand, and A. Gamoran. "Discussion-Based Approaches to Developing Understanding: Classroom Instruction and Student Performance in Middle and High School English." *American Educational Research Journal* 40, no. 3 (2003): 685–730.

Atwell, Nancie. *In the Middle: New Understandings about Writing, Reading, and Learning.* 2nd ed. Portsmouth, NH: Heinemann, 1998.

Ball, A. and M. Farr. "Language Varieties, Culture, and Teaching the English Language Arts." In *Handbook of Research on Teaching English Language Arts*, edited by J. M. Jensen, 435–45. 2nd ed. Mahwah, NJ: Erlbaum, 2003.

Calkins, Lucy. *The Art of Teaching Writing.* Portsmouth, NH: Heinemann, 1986.

_____. *The Nuts and Bolts of Teaching Writing.* Portsmouth, NH: FirstHand, 2003.

_____. *Units of Study for Primary Writing: A Yearlong Curriculum.* Portsmouth, NH: FirstHand, 2003.

Collins, Allan, John Seely Brown, and Susan E. Newman. *Cognitive Apprenticeship: Teaching the Craft of Reading, Writing and Mathematics.* Cambridge, MA: Bolt Beranek and Newman, 1989.

Common Core State Standards for English Language Arts & Literacy in History/Social Studies, Science, and Technical Subjects. S.l.: Common Core Standards Initiative, 2012.

Cremin, Teresa. "Creativity, Uncertainty and Discomfort: Teachers as Writers." *Cambridge Journal of Education* (2006): 415–33.

Culham, Ruth. *6 + 1 Traits of Writing: The Complete Guide Grades 3 and Up.* New York: Scholastic Professional Books, 2003.

Daniels, Harvey and Steven Zemelman. *A Writing Project: Training Teachers of Composition from Kindergarten to College.* Portsmouth, NH: Heinemann Educational Books, 1985.

Daniels, Harvey, Steven Zemelman, and Nancy Steineke. *Content-area Writing: Every Teacher's Guide.* Portsmouth, NH: Heinemann, 2007.

Dorn, Linda J. and Carla Soffos. *Scaffolding Young Writers: A Writer's Workshop Approach.* Portland, ME: Stenhouse, 2001.

Duke, Nell K. and V. Susan Bennett-Armistead. *Reading & Writing Informational Text in the Primary Grades. New York: Scholastic Teaching Resources, 2003.*

Fisher, Bobbi. *Thinking and Learning Together: Curriculum and Community in a Primary Classroom.* Portsmouth, NH: Heinemann, 1995.

Fisher, Douglas and Nancy Frey. "Writing Instruction for Struggling Adolescent Readers: A Gradual Release Model." *Journal of Adolescent and Adult Literacy* 46 (2003): 396–407.

Fisher, Douglas, Nancy Frey, and Carol Rothenberg. *Content-area Conversations: How to Plan Discussion-based Lessons for Diverse Language Learners.* Alexandria, VA: Association for Supervision and Curriculum Development, 2008.

Fletcher, Ralph J. and JoAnn Portalupi. *Craft Lessons: Teaching Writing K–8.* 2nd ed. Portland, ME: Stenhouse Publishers, 2007.

Gallagher, Kelly. *Write Like This: Teaching Real-world Writing through Modeling & Mentor Texts.* Portland, ME: Stenhouse Publishers, 2011.

Graves, Donald H. *A Fresh Look at Writing.* Portsmouth, NH: Heinemann, 1994.

_____. *How to Catch a Shark, and Other Stories About Teaching and Learning.* Portsmouth, NH: Heinemann, 1998.

_____. *Writing: Teachers and Children at Work.* Exeter, NH: Heinemann Educational Books, 1983.

Harwayne, Shelley. *Writing through Childhood: Rethinking Process and Product.* Portsmouth, NH: Heinemann, 2001.

Howard, Mary. *Good to Great Teaching: Focusing on the Literacy Work That Matters.* Portsmouth, NH: Heinemann, 2012.

Hoyt, Linda and Kelly Boswell. *Crafting Nonfiction Intermediate: Lessons on Writing Process, Traits, and Craft.* Portsmouth, NH: Heinemann, 2012.

Hoyt, Linda and Teresa Therriault. *Mastering the Mechanics: Ready-to-Use Lessons for Modeled, Guided, and Independent Editing.* New York: Scholastic, 2008.

Kaag, John. "The Perfect Essay." *The New York Times*, May 15, 2014, Opinion sec. http://opinionator.blogs.nytimes.com/2014/05/05/the-perfect-essay/?_php=true&_type=blogs&_php=true&_type=blogs&_php=true&_type=blogs&_r=2& (accessed August 8, 2014).

Kaplan, Avi. "Clarifying Metacognition, Self-Regulation, and Self-Regulated Learning: What's the Purpose?" *Educational Psychology Review* (2008), 477–84.

Kittle, Penny. *Write Beside Them: Risk, Voice, and Clarity in High School Writing.* Portsmouth, NH: Heinemann, 2008.

Lane, Barry. *Reviser's Toolbox.* Shoreham, VT: Discover Writing Press, 1999.

Le Guin, Ursula K. *Dancing at the Edge of the World: Thoughts on Words, Women, Places.* New York: Grove Press, 1989.

Mason, Pamela A. and Emily Phillips Galloway. "Let Them Talk!" *Reading Today*, 2012.

Moore, Elizabeth. "An Interview with Educator and Author Chris Lehman." Two Writing Teachers. http://twowritingteachers.wordpress.com/2014/09/08/so-what-does-it-take-to-be-a-great-writing-teacher/ (accessed May 20, 2014).

Murray, Donald Morison and Thomas Newkirk. *The Essential Don Murray: Lessons from America's Greatest Writing Teacher.* Portsmouth, NH: Boynton/Cook Publishers/Heinemann, 2009.

Newkirk, Thomas and Penny Kittle, editors. *Children Want to Write: Donald Graves and the Revolution in Children's Writing.* Portsmouth, NH: Heinemann, 2013.

Newkirk, Thomas. *Misreading Masculinity: Boys, Literacy, and Popular Culture.* Portsmouth, NH: Heinemann, 2002.

_____. *Understanding Writing: Ways of Observing, Learning, and Teaching.* 2nd ed. Portsmouth, NH: Heinemann, 1988.

Oczkus, Lori D. *Guided Writing: Practical Lessons, Powerful Results.* Portsmouth, NH: Heinemann, 2007.

O'Donnell-Allen, Cindy. "The Best Writing Teachers Are Writers Themselves." *The Atlantic,* September 26, 2012.

Pearson, P. D. and L. Fielding. "Comprehension Instruction." In *Handbook of Reading Research,* edited by R. Barr, M. L. Kamil, P. B. Mosenthal, and P. D. Pearson, 815–60. Vol. 2. White Plains, NY: Longman, 1991.

Pearson, P. D. and M. C. Gallagher. "The Instruction of Reading Comprehension." *Contemporary Educational Psychology* 8 (1983): 317–44.

Peters, Gerhard and John T. Wooley. "Theodore Roosevelt: Address to the New York State Agricultural Association, Syracuse, NY." Theodore Roosevelt: Address to the New York State Agricultural Association, Syracuse, NY. http://www.presidency.ucsb.edu/ws/?pid=24504 (accessed August 8, 2014).

Portalupi, JoAnn and Ralph Fletcher. *Nonfiction Craft Lessons: Teaching Information Writing K–8.* Portland, ME: Stenhouse Publishers, 2001.

Ray, Katie Wood and Lisa B. Cleaveland. *About the Authors: Writing Workshop with Our Youngest Writers.* Portsmouth, NH: Heinemann, 2004.

Ray, Katie Wood and Lester Laminack. *The Writing Workshop: Working through the Hard Parts (and They're All Hard Parts).* Urbana, IL: National Council of Teachers of English, 2001.

Ray, Katie Wood. *What You Know by Heart: How to Develop Curriculum for Your Writing Workshop.* Portsmouth, NH: Heinemann, 2002.

_____. *Wondrous Words: Writers and Writing in the Elementary Classroom.* Urbana, IL: National Council of Teachers of English, 1999.

Routman, Regie. *Conversations: Strategies for Teaching, Learning, and Evaluating.* Portsmouth, NH: Heinemann, 2000.

_____. *Writing Essentials: Raising Expectations and Results While Simplifying Teaching.* Portsmouth, NH: Heinemann, 2005.

Safire, William. "Gifts of Gab." *The New York Times*, December 19, 2008.

Spandel, Vicki. *Creating Writers: Through 6-trait Writing Assessment and Instruction.* 4th ed. Boston: Pearson Allyn and Bacon, 2005.

_____. *Creating Young Writers: Using the Six Traits to Enrich Writing Process in Primary Classrooms.* Upper Saddle River, NJ: Pearson/Allyn and Bacon, 2004.

Stead, Tony. *Is That a Fact? Teaching Nonfiction Writing K–3.* Portland, ME: Stenhouse, 2002.

_____. *Reality Checks: Teaching Reading Comprehension with Nonfiction.* Portland, ME: Stenhouse Publishers, 2006.

Stiggins, R. "New Assessment Beliefs for a New School Mission." *Phi Delta Kappan* 86, no. 1 (2004): 22–27.

Thomas, Rick. *Whiteout! A Book About Blizzards.* Minneapolis, MN: Picture Window Books, 2005.

Tobin, Lad. *Writing Relationships: What Really Happens in the Composition Class.* Portsmouth, NH: Boynton/Cook Heinemann, 1993.

Whitmarsh, Brett. "Continuing Don Graves' legacy: 'It's going to be on you.'" http://info.heinemann.com/blog/bid/333798/Continuing-Don-Graves-legacy-It-s-going-to-be-on-you?utm_campaign=2014_S_InspiredByDon&utm_source=facebook&utm_medium=social&utm_content=3737767 (accessed January 27, 2014).

Zemelman, Steven, Harvey Daniels, and Arthur Hyde. *Best Practice: New Standards for Teaching and Learning in America's Schools.* 2nd ed. Portsmouth, NH: Heinemann, 1998.

Zinsser, William Knowlton. *On Writing Well: An Informal Guide to Writing Nonfiction.* New York: Harper & Row, 1976.

Zumbrunn, Sharon and Keegan Krause. "Conversations with Leaders: Principles of Effective Writing Instruction." *The Reading Teacher* (2012), 346–53.

Write **THIS WAY**